Coming out of homosexuality.

A true story

By

Michael Bruce

ISBN: 978-1-326-65653-9

Contents

<u>Chapter 1</u>

"Early Years."

Winchester, England. March1947:

The air outside was bitterly cold. Icicles hung like glistening daggers from the trees and telephone wires. Snow had been piled up high by the snowploughs either side of even the main roads; fields were covered in thick snow with drifts of several feet in height in many places, and many country roads were still impassable. The date was the 21st of March, officially the first day of spring, but this year the countryside in the south of England still lay in the grip of perhaps the coldest winter of the century.

A mother-to-be had been taken to a nursing-home in Winchester a few days before, to avoid being trapped by snowdrifts when her labour-pains started. Now she was in the final stages of labour, with a midwife in attendance. She was not having an easy time! It seemed that ***I did not want to be born!***

Over previous days, I had turned more than once from the correct foetal position to a feet-first position. The midwife had succeeded more than once in turning me back again, but on this final approach to the outside world, I had stubbornly reverted to what is called the "breach" position. This presented a danger of suffocation by the umbilical cord wrapping itself around my neck. Could it have been just the icy weather that I wanted to escape from? Or was it connected to my mother having been in a state of apprehension and anxiety over many weeks, prior to giving birth? She had found herself pregnant outside of wedlock, and had recently left her native country of France with her British husband-to-be. She was a stranger in a foreign land. I believe that some of this anxiety, fear and confusion had made its way into my developing senses. Now as a tiny baby, I felt unsure as to whether I was really wanted in the waiting world outside. It had felt warmer and safer, floating in the water in a dark womb. But now, despite my efforts to remain inside, I was suddenly wrenched into the brightness outside, where I gasped a lungful of air and let out my first wailing cry.

==========================

Time has passed. The place where I now found myself was old and dark, and the ladies there were severe. It felt to me like a prison, a place where you were locked up. There were other children there who seemed happy to play with toys or colour with crayons, but as for me, I was making my great escape! I don't remember how I got out. Somehow I had managed to slip out of the front door without anyone noticing. Now I was half-walking and half-running down the tree-lined road with its enormous old houses and big front gardens, frequently glancing behind me as I hurried along, fearful of being caught. I walked and I walked. I came to another road, turned left onto a steep hill, and started to walk up it. This road was steep and long; very steep and very long! It seemed quite short when Papa drove up it in his car. But I was on foot, and I was only three and a half years old!

At last I reached the top of Sleepers Hill and came to Romsey Road. I knew I had to be very careful here. This was a busy road, going downhill right down into Winchester, and even in those days there were cars, busses and lorries travelling quite fast. I managed to cross the road all by myself, walked down the hill and turned into Chilbolton Avenue. Even this big road, with its lopped trees either side, seemed to go on forever. My legs ached and my heart thumped. At last I could see Links Road up ahead on the right hand side. It was opposite the club-house where Papa went to play golf. It was different from the other roads because it was stony and full of potholes, and when it rained these would be full of water. Then I could jump in them and make a big splash, if I had my boots on! But I didn't have them on today, and anyway the potholes were dry, and my legs were hurting.

Our house looked very big. It was the first one on the right hand side, just after the pathway to the little wood. At last I had reached the front door. I couldn't reach the bell, so I banged as hard as I could. Edith, the maid, opened the door and looked shocked to see me. She ran back into the house shouting for Mama. I heard voices talking loudly. I wanted someone to pick me up and hug me, and give me something to drink. Mama came hurrying to the door, muttering; "O la la la la la la! Que va dire Donald!"

As a child, I could speak and understand French, so I knew she was saying something like, "Oh my goodness, what's Papa going to say!" I did not know this, but my absence had been reported by the playschool ladies to the police, and to Papa at his work, and now the police were out searching for this runaway little boy. Meanwhile I was left standing in the hallway while a frantic phone call was made to Papa at his office. The next few minutes were spent with Mama pacing around the hallway, talking to herself in French, while Edith disappeared out of sight. By now my body was aching and shaking and my thirst was desperate. My joy and relief to have found my way home from that prison had turned to a sick feeling of apprehension and fear. Suddenly, I heard a sound like flying pebbles as Papa's car drove into the gravel drive

4

very fast and then stopped. Papa got straight out; his face looking red and angry. Ignoring Mama who was standing in the doorway, he strode over to where I was half-hiding in the front porch behind the pillar. He shouted angrily at me that I was a very naughty boy to have run away from playschool, and for disturbing him at the office. I had caused a lot of trouble for a lot of people and I was not staying here at home. He was taking me straight back to the playschool. I do not remember receiving any physical punishment from him; just angry words followed by deep silence. I felt like a nuisance to everyone. I thought; "I must be a very bad boy."

I was soon delivered back to playschool where the ladies, who had also been reprimanded for letting me escape, were even frostier than before. By now I was tired; upset; frightened and very thirsty. I still hadn't had a drink! I hid myself away for the rest of the morning until it was time for Papa to take me home on his way back for lunch.

Already, the sense that I had at birth, that I was unwanted and unloved was being fuelled by experience. Mama was an artistic person who loved to dream of beauty and romance. She would often sit at the piano and practise singing scales in a soprano voice, as if she was the leading lady in an opera. I hated it, because her voice was loud and high and I felt ignored by her.

Papa was frightening when he got angry. He was a man of pride, ambition and drive. He seemed to be good at everything he tried to do. Yet year by year, I felt that I wasn't the kind of son he had hoped for and that there must be something very wrong with me. So I tried even harder to be quiet, to be good and to keep myself to myself.

Chapter 2

"Loss of a Mother."

Just a few months after I had run away from playschool, my brother was born. I had been told that a baby was coming into the house and I was excited to have someone to play with, as I didn't have any friends. I could see that preparations were being made. One day, Mama was taken off to the hospital, and I was told that she would be away until it was time to come home with the baby. I did not miss her too much, because I was already having other ladies staying in our house to look after me. They were referred to as "au pair" girls. When Mama did return, she brought with her my new baby brother. They named him Andrew. I was disappointed because he couldn't play with me, but just lay in his cot or cried for his bottle.

Time passed. Papa was usually out during the day-time, and sometimes evenings and nights too. His business was growing and he had moved to a bigger factory on the Industrial Estate. He now had a small group of employees in the office and the factory. He would organise, invent, sell and motivate staff, as well as visiting customers and attending sales conferences. He was advancing in the world, but Mama did not like to be left behind without him.

One day, when I was about five years old, Papa announced that he wanted to get a dog. I knew that Mama liked dogs, because I had seen photos of her taken in France before they were married, and she often had a small dog with her. So with great excitement in my heart, we drove to a place where they had some puppies for sale. Mama and Papa, with my help, chose a small bundle of black curly hair, with a little brown moustache. I loved him straight away, and he was allowed to sit with me on the back seat with a blanket over my lap, for the journey home. By the time we arrived home, both the blanket and my short-trousers felt warm and wet from his nervous "wee", but I didn't mind. As far as I was concerned, *"My dog Bruno had arrived at home"!*

Over the next year, Bruno grew into a big and very handsome dog, the size of a large Labrador. He was a cross-breed, half Airedale Terrier and half black Labrador. Papa never took him for proper walks on the lead, but Bruno was allowed to accompany him on the golf course to chase rabbits. Bruno often went missing for hours at a time. He would leave our house in the morning and return later in the day, frequently followed by a pack of his dog-friends from all over town. They were all shapes and sizes, and loved to play chasing games in our large garden, much to my delight. But not to Papa's! Bruno would leap over the flower beds, while the smaller dogs would crash straight through them, trampling Papa's plants and flowers. Bruno frequently caused annoyance to Papa by visiting the Girls' School down the road and bringing home the pupils' scarves, blouses or knickers which he loved to steal from the changing rooms. He even visited the school first thing in the morning, to be found sitting on the front row with a class-full of giggling girls when the teacher walked in. Needless to say, Papa would often receive phone calls from the school or the police, telling him to collect Bruno and reimburse money for spoiled clothing.

By the age of six, I was attending a day-school in Otterbourne, a village about four miles out of Winchester, and I was travelling on my own on two different buses. In the winter, the walk up our unmade-up road would have to be done in the dark. As I made my way up, trying not to twist my ankle in a pothole, I would hear a sound like a galloping racehorse approaching at speed. Suddenly a huge black animal would leap at me out of the darkness, nearly knocking me to the ground. His front paws reached my shoulders and his warm wet tongue licked my face. No matter how long he had been absent from home during the day, Bruno would always be back in time to meet me from school! The only exceptions were when he had been picked up as a stray dog, and locked in the police dog-pound!

I now had a "best friend", and Bruno and I spent many happy hours together. Then one fateful day, when Mama was already becoming ill, Papa announced to the family that Bruno was too much trouble for us and he would be better suited to living on a farm. A day or two later, Papa told me to say goodbye to him, and they both left in the car without me. Papa had said we could visit him on the farm, but we never did. I was heart-broken. My best friend was gone, and no-one seemed to care.

During my childhood, Papa liked to take his family on an occasional picnic by the seaside. I remember playing "cowboys and Indians" with little Andrew, paddling in the cold sea and eating jam sandwiches with bits of sand in them. Once a year in the summer-time, we would all get up in the middle of the night to make the long car journey to Cornwall. I dreaded the journey as I was always car-sick. We never got very far on the journey before Papa had to stop for me to be sick by the side of the road. This would repeat itself again during the trip, which made the journey even longer, and I felt such a nuisance.

We sometimes went to a place in Cornwall where there was a huge beach with large waves. Papa had purchased surf-boards for us to try to ride the waves lying on our stomachs. I was about seven years old, and I was enjoying paddling and trying to lie on my surf-board. I ventured out a little further into the on-coming surf to try to get a better ride. Suddenly, a very large wave knocked me over, and I landed on my hands and knees on the sand with the wave rushing over my head. It had knocked the board out of my hand. I tried to get up again, but each time another wave knocked me down again. I swallowed some sea-water and couldn't breathe. I thought I was going to drown! Still on my hands and knees, I lifted one arm as high as I could above the rushing water. Suddenly another hand grabbed my little hand and pulled me up from under the water. Papa had seen my distress and had hurried to my aid. He had saved my life! After this incident I was nervous to swim out of my depth or under water.

I was eight years old and my day-school closed suddenly; some sort of scandal among the teachers, I was told. Papa managed to find another school for me to attend. It was a few miles away in the heart of the countryside. It was a boarding school for boys aged seven to thirteen. I started at the beginning of a new term and most of the other boys already knew each other. I was scared and lonely, and I was sick every morning after breakfast. I lost about a stone in weight by the end of that first term!

Three years had now come and gone. I spent much of this time at school. I went home on occasional Sundays, just for a few hours, as well as for the holidays. Mama was often ill in bed, and one day I tried to stay with her in the bedroom. I was told that she was too ill and I had to leave her alone. I got very upset and started to cry and refused to leave the room. I had to be dragged away by force and was told that I could not visit her in her bedroom again. Meanwhile Papa would sometimes take Andrew and me for outings. In the summer of that year, he took us both camping for a night or two in the New Forest. He towed a caravan behind his car and set up everything in a field. At bed-time Andrew had the little bed and I was allowed to sleep next to Papa in the double bed. I wanted him to hug and cuddle me but he just said good-night to us both. Then, in my nervousness at finding myself lying close to Papa, I started to twitch around in the bed and kick my legs against his without wanting to. I tried to stop it, but couldn't. Suddenly Papa got annoyed with me and said; "Right, that's enough! You keep kicking me! I want Andrew to come in this bed with me and you can sleep over there in the little bed." I swopped beds with Andrew. Then I lay in the dark feeling sad and lonely and wondering why Pop wouldn't cuddle me. "He likes Andrew, but he doesn't like me," I thought to myself.

A week or two later I was back at boarding school. By now I often felt happier at school than at home. One autumn morning, I was sitting at a desk in the middle of a lesson, when the headmaster walked into our classroom. He spoke to the teacher and pointed at me. Calling me by my surname, he told me to come with him to his study straight away. I was frightened and embarrassed wondering what I might have done wrong. But the headmaster didn't look angry.

"Your father is coming here to talk to you," he said quietly. "Wait by the main entrance until you see his car arrive". Again I was scared. Why was Papa coming here on a weekday morning? After a few minutes I saw Papa's car coming up the driveway and into the courtyard in front of the school building. Papa did not get out of his car, but waited for me to walk out to him. He seemed very solemn, and told me that he wanted to drive up the lane to a quiet spot where he could park. It didn't take long for him to find a suitable entrance to a field and Papa pulled in and stopped. Still I had no idea why we were there. Then Papa turned and spoke; "Mama has died!" he blurted out. Then he started to sob loudly and heavily.

I was shocked. I had never been told that she was dying, although I had wondered about it. Also I had never seen Papa cry or show any weakness. Suddenly in my young emotions there arose not grief, but a kind of despising anger. All the rejection and pain surfaced in me. While he sat sobbing, I wanted to open the car door and run away. I wanted to tell him that I hated him and that I never wanted to see him again. With all my effort I managed to hold down these feelings, and I sat in the car next to him in total silence without shedding a single tear. After a minute or two, Papa managed to compose himself. "I will have to take you back to school now," he said.

So within just a few minutes of leaving the school entrance, I was walking back in again on my own, and Papa's car was disappearing down the long driveway. My anger had been stuffed down inside of me, and now I just felt numb. The news about Mama's death had been buried somewhere deep inside. Quite soon I began to feel that she had never existed. All memories vanished somewhere in my mind, where I could no longer reach them. I was not taken to her funeral as this was not considered a good idea for children in those days, so I had no opportunity to grieve.

During the next days and weeks the Headmaster and his wife were concerned about me. Not because I was constantly bursting into tears and sobbing, but because I was not doing so. In fact I seemed to continue the term as if nothing had happened. Could it be that I took Mama's death as a final rejection both by her, but also by "Woman" as a whole? Somewhere in my heart I vowed never to trust or get close to a woman again.

Just a little while after Mama's death, I had a strange experience. It was a Sunday, and all the boys were crammed into the tiny school chapel, attending the morning service. This was compulsory for us and while some hated it, I had always liked to hear about God and Jesus, even though my family did not regularly attend church. I was sitting in the front row of the little chapel and we were singing the last hymn. After that we were expected to sit or kneel for the closing prayer and benediction.

I sat down and tried to pray in my heart, when suddenly I felt as if I was all alone in the chapel. Yet I was not alone! In front of me there was a person, but I couldn't see him. He was invisible but I could *feel* him, not by touch but by emotion. I felt wrapped in a blanket of love; deep love; comforting love; out-of-this world love. I felt like I was being held in strong fatherly arms yet cradled like a baby by his mother. All this happened in less than a minute.

Suddenly I was aware of noise around me as the other boys stood up to file out of chapel. The person and the feeling of love were gone. I didn't know if I had felt the presence of Jesus himself, or of one of his angels, but I knew I had been visited by someone from Heaven, and in the days ahead, no matter how dark they became, I always had a belief in my heart that God was real, and that Heaven truly existed.

Back at home in Winchester, Andrew was now seven years old, and still at a day school. I would only see him during the holidays. Papa had thrown himself into work and business to combat his grief. Yet within eighteen months of Mama's death, he had met a widow with two children, and had re-married. Now I had a new step-mother who I agreed to call "mummy", a step-brother of nearly thirteen and a grown-up step-sister of nineteen who had already left home to train as a nurse.

Chapter 3

"Developing Sexuality."

It was Easter 1959, and I had just turned twelve years old. My boyish face was looking more mature and my body was rapidly gaining extra height. My voice sounded squeaky one minute and deep another minute, and it wasn't long before I had to stop singing in the school choir. One night as I was sleeping, I had a dream which was accompanied by some strange but very pleasurable feelings. When I awoke from this dream, to my shock and surprise, I found there was something wet and sticky on my stomach and my pyjamas. I felt worried and anxious that there was something wrong with me; I knew next to nothing about puberty. Fortunately some of the boys in my dormitory, though less physically mature than me, were more street-wise than I was. When I shared what had just happened to me that night, some boys were baffled but others started to giggle and laugh. Then one boy said; "You've had a wet-dream! Now you're going to be able to have sex with girls!"

I still had a look of confusion and fear on my face; another boy who had an older sister, tried to tell me about the "birds and the bees." But the suggestion of having sex with a girl didn't seem to carry any interest or excitement for me. Instead, I was noticing a desire to look at the naked bodies of some of the other boys when they were dressing or undressing at bath time or at the swimming pool. I wanted to touch them and be touched by them. But none of the other boys seemed to feel that way about me!

It wasn't long before the same thing happened again in my sleep, and I soon discovered that I could give myself those pleasant feelings in the daytime too, by masturbation. In those days at boarding-school, boys often wrestled with each other, either in the dormitory or in the school grounds. Many of these fights held no particular interest for me, but it would be very different if the boys involved were physically attractive to me. My heartbeat would start to race and my body would shake with excitement, as I watched them rolling over each other until one boy succeeded in pinning the other down. The more intense the fight, the more excited I would get, and afterwards I would feel such a sexual stimulation that I would hurry to a toilet and masturbate. On other occasions I would use my imagination to re-create the fights between certain boys and even imagine myself being pinned by one of them.

The school building was large and rambling; it had been a beautiful manor house in its heyday. The dormitories were spread about on various corridors on the upstairs floor, each one with a stuffed head of a wild African animal mounted on the wall. I was sleeping in the dormitory called "Rhino" with a massive rhino head mounted right above my bed! This dormitory, for boys in their final year, was located at the end of a quiet corridor at the far side of the building. Outside the dormitory there was a passage with a linen-cupboard and a small wash-room with toilet next to it. This linen-cupboard was the place where matron's staff kept the boys' clothes that had been washed and were ready to issue on bath-nights. In my desperation for touch and self-excitement I would sometimes sneak along there in the daytime, open the cupboard, and take out some underwear. All clothes were labelled with the name of the boy who owned them, and my excitement was to "borrow" the underwear belonging to a boy whom I found attractive, and try them on in the toilet next-door. As I did so I would imagine myself wrestling with him and I would masturbate. It was only a matter of time before I would get caught.

14

Sure enough on one such occasion, I was just putting the underwear back in the cupboard as neatly as I could, when a housekeeper came along the corridor to put away some more clean washing. She asked me what my name was, and what was I doing there? I stammered out some feeble excuse, feeling flushed in the face with fear and embarrassment. It wasn't long before I was called to the Headmaster's study again. When I got there, anticipating the punishment of six strokes from the cane, I was surprised to find the headmaster's wife and matron there too. I tried to make excuses or tell lies about my behaviour, but it was clear that they had already guessed what I had been doing. What I had not realised was that these adults were actually very concerned about this boy who had lost his mother; a boy who had shown no obvious grief or other emotional reaction but was now displaying secretive sexual behaviour. I had been recognised as an emotionally disturbed boy who must be treated with special care, and a psychiatrist had advised the school that I should not be given corporal punishment, but that alternative disciplinary measures should be found. By now, I had added shame and guilt on top of rejection and loneliness. I never resorted to that cupboard again but my attraction to other boys grew stronger and the wrestling interest stayed with me.

Meanwhile in the classroom, I was struggling to concentrate on my studies and was often receiving poor marks. Papa had been warned by the headmaster that I might fail my exams to a Public School and might have to be sent to a "special-needs" school for emotionally disturbed children. But mysteriously, during my final year towards the exams, my concentration began to improve, my marks got better and, that summer, my exam results in all except Maths were good enough to achieve an above-average pass mark. Papa was relieved and he informed me that I would be starting at Bradfield College in Berkshire, at the start of the autumn term.

Chapter 4

"Sexuality Confirmed"

One morning in early September, I woke up with butterflies in my stomach and a mixed sense of fear and excitement. The school summer-holidays had drawn to a close and the day had arrived for "Pop", as our extended family now called him, to drive me to my new school. A large trunk, like the sort used for long sea voyages, had been packed with my belongings; all the items you might need for a long stay far away from home. The journey to the school seemed very long even though it lasted less than an hour. Eventually, we arrived at the village of Bradfield. It seemed little more than a few houses, a village shop and post office and a red telephone kiosk. At the bottom of the hill there were several large grey school buildings, forming a square called the "Quadrangle". On one side there was even a church! This was in fact the school chapel, but compared to my previous school chapel, it looked like a large church. After a brief tour by car of the main school buildings, Pop drove back up the steep hill and turned into the driveway at the top. On the side of the driveway there was a sign which read, "House on the Hill." This was to become my second home for the next four years.

There was plenty of activity going on. Other cars were arriving and leaving with parents bringing their sons to school. Some boys were arriving for the first time, while others seemed happy to be back amongst school-friends. We had to register my arrival and unload the trunk and there were helpers on hand to show people around and also to the dormitory where the new-boys like me would be sleeping. I was accompanied to a large upstairs room with a wooden floor and big windows. In this dormitory there were ten or twelve metal beds and some cupboards. Thankfully there were no animal heads on the walls. After unpacking my trunk, I was told that there would be a "Welcome Meeting" in the afternoon for all the new boys, taking place down in the main school. It was time for Pop to leave now. He bid me goodbye and left in his car.

Suddenly I was all alone in a strange new place. The "Welcome Meeting" was helpful in explaining about the school; then supper back at the House on the Hill gave me a chance to see and meet the other boys. All the new boys looked worried and nervous like I was. I was keen to find a friend. Later that evening we all had to go to our dormitories. Mine was for new boys, so we received another welcome and instructions from a tall, much older boy with ginger hair. He introduced himself as the "head of house" that year, and he was accompanied by a stocky middle-aged man who was introduced as our "housemaster." We were given lots of rules and regulations to be followed and obeyed, but I was too nervous to take them all in. That night, I slept fitfully as I tried to adjust to my new environment.

The next morning after breakfast, the new boys were told about the "Bumph Test." We had each been allocated a boy from the year above to be our "nurse," to show us around the whole school and the classrooms, and also to teach us the rules and the punishments for not keeping them. The test involved learning a great deal of information about the school; the names of teachers and the subjects they taught; the nicknames for various roads, landmarks and local places; the colours of various school ties, and so on. It seemed like an endless list! The pass-mark was apparently set very high, and the punishment for failing to reach it was that your "nurse" received six-of-the-best with the cane from the head of house for not having taught you properly. Whether these threats were true or not, I could not be sure. But for me, being nervous and sensitive, this test loomed over me like a giant black cloud. Great anxiety was now mixed with the feelings of fear and abandonment with which I was already struggling. I was filled with dread! It wasn't long before I was standing in the old red telephone box down in the village sobbing and begging Pop and Mum to come back and take me home! Mum was quite distressed and I think she would have collected me. But Pop knew better. Using his army training and strength of character, he told me that I had to learn to face things like this in life. So nobody came to fetch me. He did the right thing. In the end, the bumph test wasn't so bad and we had two weeks to learn it all. I passed the test and nobody got the cane.

Once lessons were underway, I started to settle into a routine and make friends with some of the boys in my year-group. Inevitably, one or two of them were attractive to me, so I hung around them first for comfort. There was no fighting or wrestling allowed in the dormitories at this school but after "lights-out" there were some furtive movements between beds and giggling amongst some of the boys. But no-one ever tried to come near me in my bed. By the time I turned fourteen, I was already looking quite manly. I liked to do press-ups in the dormitory and pull-ups on a steel railing in the changing rooms. I was tall and quite muscular for my age and was becoming hirsute on my chest. I didn't want to look like that; inside I wanted to be cute and skinny so that other boys might fancy me!

A year had passed. Another set of new-boys arrived and amongst them was Billy! He was thirteen and had short, gingery-blond hair and blue eyes. He had not reached puberty yet and looked young for his age. To my eyes he was very cute and I found myself developing a crush on him. Over the next year or two, as Billy matured, I often longed to hold him in my arms and have bodily contact. He knew I had a crush on him and would sometimes flirt with me and let me put my arm around him, but this was as far as it would go. I was desperate for love and sexual contact, but I never pushed myself on him against his will.

By this time, many of the boys of my age were talking about girls and girl-friends who they met during the holidays. Magazines and naughty pictures were being shown around when it was safe to do so. I was realising that I was different from the others. Girls and naughty pictures of them held no interest or excitement for me. In fact the exact opposite was true; I felt a sense of revulsion towards them. My sexual interest in boys seemed firmly stuck!

Chapter 5

"Finishing the School-years."

By now, another passion was growing in me – pop music! I managed to persuade Pop to buy me a guitar for my birthday. It was a shiny white semi-acoustic guitar with an electric pick-up and a lead for an amplifier. I loved this guitar and taught myself a few simple chords; soon I started writing songs with it. By the start of 1963, as I was reaching sixteen, there was a revolution in British pop music. First the Beatles, then the Searchers and many other groups emerged from Liverpool and the North. Soon groups and solo singers from towns and cities all over the country started hitting the charts. I was inspired by this music and wanted to be part of it.

There was another boy at school whose parents lived in a village near Winchester. He played the drums and his name was Sam. Soon we had formed a group at school and one Sunday it was the turn of Sam's dad to collect us by car to come home for the day. I had cut my hair at the front with a Beatle fringe. Sam's dad dropped me at the end of the drive of the house in the country where Pop and Mum now lived. I walked up the drive to the front door expecting a nice welcome. But when Pop opened the door, he looked at my new haircut and exclaimed: "You're not coming in here looking like that! Go back down the drive and do something about your hair!"

I walked back down the drive like a puppy with its tail between its legs after a scolding. I felt very hurt and rejected. I brushed my hair back with my hand to try to get rid of the offending fringe. When I came back to the door a minute or two later I had become acceptable for admission, but another nail of rejection had been driven into my heart.

Music became an important part of my life. Although I had no training, apart from a few piano lessons as a small boy, I enjoyed a wide range of music but had never learned to read sheet music. In the school holidays I would record my compositions on a tape recorder and send them off by post to music publishers in London. One morning at school the housemaster was passing out letters for the boys during breakfast. A small slim package addressed to me was handed out. It had been forwarded on from home. Not knowing what it was, I opened it in front of the other boys on my table. Inside was a "Single." (a 45 rpm record.) To my amazement, I looked at the "A" side, and it read: "I want to be free" by Whichwhat.

Below the title and the group's name was the name of the composer. It was my name! One of my songs had been recorded without me even knowing about it. The record itself was a little disappointing and met with no success, but suddenly I had become a published songwriter and my ego was inflated by the sudden admiration of my friends. I was still playing in a school group and Pop did not approve. At home he would tell me that I was mixing with the wrong type of boys.

However, Pop was pleased that, like himself in his youth, I had developed a talent in athletics, particularly in the "220" and "440" yard sprints. In my final year I had been picked for the school team, and one event stands out in my memory. The team had travelled by coach to a famous school called "Eton," and I was running in the "440." We had taken a group of our supporters and amongst them was Billy. By now, he was about sixteen but I still had strong feelings for him. The race was about to start and I had drawn the outside lane, which I hated. The starting gun went off! I didn't want to make the mistake of going too fast too soon. But, to my dismay as I ran down the back straight, I was overtaken by both Eton boys and my own team member. As I rounded the last bend on the outside lane I could see the final straight to the finishing line but I was still trailing at the back of the pack. As I dug deep to sprint for the line, to my surprise, the other three boys began to tire and slow down. They had all started too fast. I passed all three in the final few yards to win the race. Of course our supporters were cheering me on, and after the race I was the hero of the moment. Amongst those admiring my efforts was Billy. I felt elated! My self-worth was poor so I relished some attention and admiration from my peer-group.

During my final year, Pop came to the school to have a meeting with my housemaster about my future career. I had to wait outside to start with while the two men talked together. Then I was called into the study and asked to sit down. Pop spoke first; "We have been discussing what career you might want to follow and we have decided on accountancy," he said confidently. My marks in maths over the years had been poor, so I imagined that this comment was a joke to set me more at ease. I laughed nervously. But from the look on their faces I quickly realised that this was not supposed to be a joke. By this time my personal hopes and ambitions were directed towards seeking success, money and fame through pop-music. As my face fell and my stomach knotted I heard Pop continue; "Of course you'll never make a living out of your pop-music. You must have a proper professional career; and if you're going to join the family business one day, then accountancy would be very useful, as you're no good at science or engineering." I had no will to resist. I thought to myself that I should do what Pop wanted, but still follow my song-writing ambitions in my own time.

During the last summer holidays before leaving school I went to Devon with three other school friends. I had recently passed my driving test and, since none of us owned a car, Pop allowed us to use a spare car from his business. We were going to be camping, so we managed to cram tents and belongings into the car as well as ourselves. We drove down to Devon.

Devon has many narrow winding roads. I was driving down a narrow lane and I could see the lane continuing up the hill on the other side of the valley. All four of us were in the car and I was driving quite fast. At the bottom of the hill I could see a farm building with a stone wall jutting out into the lane which had an "S" shaped bend, before continuing up the hill on the other side. As I approached this bend, it reminded me of a chicane on a race track and I thought it would be fun to take it at speed. With only a very short distance remaining before reaching the bend, suddenly and without warning, the front of a large farm tractor emerged from the other side of the lane, right opposite the farmhouse wall. It was coming from an entrance to a field that had been hidden from view by a tall hedge. I was confronted with a stone wall to my left and a big metal machine on my right with not enough room in between. There was no time to stop. In my thoughts I said, "God, help us!" Then I shut my eyes, expecting a horrible noise of crunching stone and metal, followed by serious injury if not death. Moments later, I opened my eyes again. I could hardly believe what I saw. We were travelling up the hill on the other side of the bend. As I glanced in my rear-view mirror I could see the farmhouse behind me with the tractor still blocking most of the road. My friends thought that I had used an amazing piece of driving skill to take us through the obstacles and round the "S" bend, but I knew that my eyes had been shut, awaiting the inevitable impact. I remembered the visit I had received a few years earlier in the school chapel. I thought to myself that we must have been rescued by an angel of God, and somehow transported over the roadblock.

A day or two later, we were by the sea and we saw a sign for a sailing boat for hire. The charge seemed very reasonable and since two of my friends claimed to have had some sailing experience we hired the boat for an hour. Our plan was to potter about in the shelter of the bay, but I was a little anxious following the episode when I nearly drowned as a child. But, not wishing to look foolish in front of my friends I agreed to go too. At first it was quite pleasant as the water was calm. Then very quickly black clouds rolled in and the wind rose sharply. We found ourselves being driven further out to sea. As the wind grew stronger and the waves grew bigger we started to panic and fear for our lives. The main sail ripped and we lost all control of the boom which swung dangerously from side to side across the boat. At one point all four of us were hanging out over the waves on one side of the boat while water was coming in over the other side. I prayed for help again. Gradually the storm eased. There was an outboard motor but it refused to start, so we managed to use two oars to row back to the shore. It was late when we got back and we were wet, cold and frightened. The man who hired us the boat was not happy at all, but he realised that the boat was in poor condition and that we might have died out there in the bay. He sent us away and took no further action. The rest of the holiday was uneventful and we returned home safely. I decided to say nothing about our incident with the car.

Soon it was time for me to return to school and I had the opportunity of seeing my brother Andrew, now aged thirteen, start his first term at the same school. At the end of the winter term of 1964, aged seventeen, I left Bradfield College. I spent Christmas at home and at the beginning of January, after just two weeks break from school, I started work in an office in the centre of Winchester. Pop had made all the arrangements; I don't recall even attending an interview. Now I was entering into a five year "articles" in chartered accountancy with a well-known local firm. It was on-the-job practical training, with three exams along the way.

Chapter 6

"Work and Play."

On my first day at the office, I was taken by one of the secretaries to be introduced to the two partners in the firm. I was told that they must be referred to as "Sir". This was no problem to me, since I had been used to doing this when addressing the teachers at school. After a quick introduction, I was led upstairs to the top floor of the old building and into a smallish room. There were three desks in the middle of the room, two opposite one-another and one across the end. There were cupboards around two walls, a window, and lots of files and papers lying all over the place. I felt rather nervous.

I was greeted first by Rick, a tall bespectacled man in his late thirties, with an Australian accent. He was referred to as a "senior", as he had been working there for a number of years. I was shown to the empty desk and chair where I was to sit and I was introduced to the other person in the room, seated at the desk opposite mine. As he stood up to shake my hand, I was immediately struck by his deep melancholy brown eyes. His name was Paul, and I was attracted to him straight away. Although Paul was not gay, we shared many interests. He liked similar music to me and played bass guitar in a local group. Paul was also keen on motorbikes, fast cars and motor racing.

Soon, with the help of an advance twenty-first birthday present, I was able to buy my first car. It was a 1957 ex-police van. Its' former owner, a mechanic with the police, had given it a full make-over with an engine tune-up, lowered suspension, side-windows, metallic blue paint, wide road wheels, straight-through exhaust system and other accessories. To me, it was everything an aspiring boy-racer like me could ask for. This car became my faithful friend for three years. As well as being my every-day transport, I also took part with it at motor racing events called sprints and hill-climbs. Paul also competed at these events, which we often attended together, but unlike me, he was never satisfied with the cars he owned. Over the years he would sell a car and buy another almost every two months; they were often beautiful cars that most people would love to have owned.

Paul knew that I was gay and that I was attracted to him. He took advantage of my feelings for him by letting me pay for drinks and food when we went out places together. Once again my emotions were caught up in a one-sided relationship and I felt deeply lonely and un-appreciated. Paul would date girls, and even got engaged at one point, but as with cars, he soon tired of his relationships and would be looking for the next one. Of course I found this very painful, as I felt I was in love with him.

Over the late-teenage years and into my twenties, I did make my own attempts at relationships with girls. Earlier on in my teens, I had met a girl at a party who I took out a few times. She was small and skinny with a short haircut, and she looked a bit like a twelve year old boy. She seemed as nervous of boys as I was of girls, so holding hands together was about our limit! One time I took her to the cinema. It was a 12+ rating. To our huge embarrassment, a cinema attendant asked us to leave because they thought she was under-age. That was the last time we dated. Later, I also dated another girl who was completely different. As I was driving her home in my car, she started to rub my leg and undo my trouser zip. I stopped the car in a quiet spot and tried to kiss her and touch her body. She responded willingly, but instead of arousal, a feeling of revulsion came over me and I wanted to escape as soon as possible. She must have wondered what was wrong with me, and I never saw her again. A similar thing happened to me when I was playing with my group, the "Peasant Breed." We had reformed after finishing school with three new members from another school. I was the lead-singer, and we sometimes attracted girl fans at gigs. On one occasion, I was travelling in the back of someone's car, sitting between two girls. To my surprise, both girls started to fondle me and undo my trousers. I felt the same feelings of revulsion and panic as I had known before. Much to the frustration of the girls, I resisted their advances and told them to leave me alone.

During the five years of my first job, I was living at home with Mum and Pop. My step-brother was away at university and Andrew was at boarding school. At first, Pop was giving me lifts into work and back on his way to his factory, but soon I had my own car. Up till now I had not really been aware that there were other "ordinary" guys who were gay. I imagined that all gay men were very effeminate and camp. But one day, by chance, I overheard some people joking about a pub in Winchester where gay men sometimes hung out. I was curious to find out more, so one evening I went along nervously to this pub. I bought myself a soft drink and sat down on my own at a small table near the door. There were men and women of various ages in the pub and everything looked very normal. Then I noticed a young man in his early twenties glancing over at me and smiling. I smiled back. To my surprise, he came over and asked if he could sit at my table. I felt awkward but curious and we made small talk for a while. I still believed that I was not attractive to other men, so when he asked if I'd like to go and see his flat, I wondered if he was just being sociable. But once we had arrived at his flat, he sat down next to me, put his hand on my thigh, and I realised that he did have sexual intentions towards me. This was my first encounter with another gay guy, though unfortunately, I wasn't attracted to him very much. Still I had discovered that there were other ordinary guys with similar feelings to me and that some gay men could be attracted to me.

My parents sometimes went away for a night or two, or even longer on holiday. I would be left in the house by myself. I had begun to answer adverts to meet other guys; I had also found both a pub and a club in Southampton where gay men met together. I started to invent excuses for going out late, especially on a Saturday night. If my parents were away, I would occasionally invite someone back to the house.

One time I drove to London to meet a black guy who had advertised for friends. He looked attractive in his photo. Sure enough, he was young, slim and had a bubbly personality and he seemed keen on me too. I spent an evening with him but I had no intentions of having any sort of permanent relationship. Unfortunately he thought otherwise, and he started writing to me with fancy-style writing on the envelopes. In one such letter he made threats of suicide if I did not agree to move in with him. My parents were becoming suspicious about these fancy-looking letters, and also about my anxious appearance and lame excuses regarding these letters. One morning Pop challenged me about it, wanting to know who was writing these letters to me. I was filled with fear and didn't know what to say, as I had been lying to them about my friends and my outings for months. I gave some feeble explanation, but that evening, I decided to write a letter to Pop, explaining that I was gay and that I had been meeting up with other men. I left this letter on the passenger seat of his car so he would see it in the morning, when he drove to work. I was in a state of fear and anxiety at work the whole day and could hardly concentrate. Later that day, after we had both arrived home, Pop got out of his chair in the living room and asked me to accompany him into the dining room. I was very nervous and scared. I sat down, wondering if Pop was going to shout at me in anger, but instead he seemed quite calm and controlled.

"Thank you for your letter," he said, speaking in a quieter voice than usual. "I must admit that Mum and I did have our suspicions about you. However, I came across this sort of thing in the army during the war, so I know how to cure you of all this. You have to promise me that you will have no further meetings with other men for the next six months, and after that you should be cured!" Well, I didn't really believe him, but I did manage to obey this command for the next six months or so. But of course, that didn't stop my thoughts and fantasies. Then there was Paul in the office; over the next few months my attraction to him just grew stronger.

After the six months had passed, I gradually returned to my former ways. I had to be very careful as I didn't want a repeat of what had happened before. I had discovered that there were other young gay men who also enjoyed wrestling, so I would arrange to meet some of these guys. I would select the ones I found attractive and, from time to time, I would arrange a wrestling meeting, using the spare bedroom at home when my parents were away. Although I took part in these wrestling sessions, I have to admit that my main aim was to take photographs of the other guys as they were wrestling in underpants or swimming trunks. I found this sexually exciting and would later use the photos for my own sexual fantasies.

Still attempting to be attracted to girls, I made contact with a girl through an advertisement. She wasn't exactly a prostitute, but she was looking for a man for sex. When I explained that I was gay and that I wanted to try to have sex with a woman, she was happy to oblige. We met in town one evening when my parents were away and she came back to the house for the night. I did not actually fancy her, but she was very experienced sexually and succeeded in seducing me to the point that we had protected sex together. I was encouraged, but still knew that there was something missing in me as far as physical attraction to women was concerned. She had been attracted to me and to my non-abusive behaviour towards her, and she wanted to see me again and start a relationship. But I declined apologetically. I felt bad that I had used her for an experiment on my sexuality.

Chapter 7

"Return Ticket to London."

I was now 22 years old and the time had come for me to sit my final exam. Pop had once again sent me on a residential crammer course for six weeks beforehand, as I struggled to learn everything on my own from study books. I sat the exam in Bristol, accompanied by another guy from my firm, and I found some of the papers difficult. I had to return to the office for a few more weeks until the results arrived. When the postman came with the letter, I was very surprised to discover that I had passed the exam and that I had now qualified as an accountant. Pop was delighted, but in my heart I still yearned for success in the music business.

Now that my five years of training had been completed, it was time to decide what to do next. Pop had been grooming me for his business, but seemed happy to let me gain some practical work experience first. I looked for an accounting job in the London area. I figured that I could take a clerical job that was not too stressful, and try to break into the music business at the same time. Added to this, I imagined that London would offer me more chance of meeting other guys, and maybe the special person that I longed for. To a degree, these aims were realised. Firstly I obtained a job in the accounts department of a large building company in the suburbs of London. The job was routine, but the pay was good, and I was happy to have a job which was straight-forward. I rented a room in a guest-house, which offered bed and communal breakfast for the six residents. I had written some songs over the previous year or so, and now I continued to write some more. I had my guitar,

31

some percussion instruments and an old four-track tape recorder, and I took my demo tapes around a few publishers and record companies. To my excitement, one small record company offered to sign me up and pay for me to record an album. With just five musicians and a very low budget, we recorded about twelve songs. These recordings were intended to be for demonstration purposes, but the record company decided to use the songs as they were. So my album was later released. They also released a single from the album. Nothing much happened as far as sales were concerned, but I had achieved a step towards my ambitions.

After six months at the building company, I was offered a new job in central London working for the accounts department of a large record company. This too was an easy clerical job. I left my room in the suburbs and found a flat-share in North London. I lived about six months here. During this time I met some guys, but I didn't much like the gay clubs or pubs in London. I never got to meet a guy that I really liked and life was rather lonely. Then, after a year away from home, Pop asked me to come to see him at his house. "It's time for you to decide whether you are going to join the family business," he said. "I need an accountant for the company. If you don't join now, I will have to find somebody else, and then you may never be part of the business."

I realised from this subtle command that I really didn't have much option. Pop had invested money into my training so that I could be part of his company. Besides which, I was not very happy in London. I figured I could still write songs and record again while working in Winchester. So I left my flat and my job in London to move back to the family home. Moving back in with my parents was a bit of a shock after doing my own thing in London! I started work with the family business at the beginning of 1971.

The situation at work proved very difficult for me. Unlike my two recent jobs, where I had joined an existing team, here at the factory I was filling a new position. The bookkeeping department was efficiently run by a middle-aged woman and her staff of three ladies. She seemed to resent the arrival of the boss's son as the accountant and she was not keen to co-operate with me. Worse still, I didn't really know what I was supposed to do in this new post! Fortunately the firm of accountants who prepared the financial accounts started me off with the keeping of monthly management records. This was in the days before desk-top computers. I often found myself sitting in my office on my own with nothing to do. Thoughts of uselessness and failure crowded into my mind and I became anxious and depressed. Some mornings I could hardly get out of my bed because of the anxiety within, and I would feel physically sick before driving to work. At other times, I would drive past a factory, a farm or a shop and tell myself that I could never do that job. I was having a crisis of self-worth, and depression was hounding me. My only relief was to fantasize about guys, and hope to meet someone special. Even song-writing was impossible while I was crippled with anxiety.

Fortunately, about this time, Pop suggested that I should have a house of my own, and that he would lend me the deposit money. This served as a distraction for me. We found a lovely old property, quite close to the centre of town, which required renovation. Pop supplied some men from his factory to do much of the work, while I was able to do smaller jobs in my spare time, such as painting and decorating. My artistic side wanted to create a trendy bachelor pad. It took several months to complete the work, but once everything was ready, I moved out of my parent's home and into this house. I needed a mortgage, so I took in three rent-paying lodgers – one man and two girls. This situation lasted about a year, and it was difficult for me to have any private life with three other people in the house. Still, I sometimes had the house to myself at weekends.

Gradually, my situation at work was improving, as I was also now doing debt-chasing and product costing. In time, I employed an assistant and a secretary. The assistant was a young man in his early twenties. I chose him at interview because he was cute looking and gentle in character, but he proved willing and helpful to me. My young secretary too was quiet and shy, but she was reliable and hard-working. I heard, a few years later, that the two of them had got married.

I was still prone to anxiety and I had taken to reading my horoscope every day and doing biorhythms. These occult-related activities were not helpful to me, but I was desperately searching for truth, direction and peace in my life. During this time, I also had the opportunity to record two further songs as "singles". They each received some airplay, but did not make it big-time.

Meanwhile, my original lodgers had all moved on. I had advertised and had now found two young single men to share my house. These guys were not gay, but we all got on quite well. One weekend, I was alone at home when I heard the sound of someone playing the drums close-by. I was curious, so went out of the front door and walked in the direction of the sound. Halfway down the narrow street there was a garage door which was open, and inside was a young man playing a drum-kit. I smiled at him and he smiled back. Then, to my surprise, he stopped playing and came out into the street to talk to me. He was in his early twenties and I was attracted to him immediately. I told him my name, and he introduced himself as Dougie. We talked for a few minutes in the street and I mentioned that I had played in a group and that I had made a record. He seemed impressed and asked if he could listen to it.

Dougie came back to my house and I played him my first single. He was very friendly and enthusiastic, with a boyish charm that was very attractive to me. We seemed to be getting on so well that I soon plucked up the courage to tell him that I was gay. To my disappointment he said that he wasn't gay, but he did seem to like my attention. Over the coming weeks and months I became infatuated with him and would see him or speak on the phone every day. He liked my company and would even go with me to the gay club, hold my hand and take part in disco-dancing with me. This situation was exciting, but also very frustrating, as I appeared to have a boyfriend, but the feelings of sexual attraction were one-sided. We took holidays together to Scotland and later to France. I gave Dougie driving lessons, bought him clothes and presents and we became very close. After holiday trips together, he would return to his parent's house and I would suddenly feel very isolated and depressed. I even felt a little suicidal once or twice. Then Dougie found a girlfriend and later became engaged. Of course, it caused me some heartache to see them out together.

When Dougie and I used to go out together on a Saturday night we would often go to a regular disco club first, and then to the gay club. Sometimes, other friends came too. They would be hoping to dance with girls at the disco, and later would have a bit of a giggle at the gay club. On one such occasion, after Dougie's engagement had been announced, we went as a group on a guy's night-out. When we reached the gay club I had some disco-dances with Dougie, while the others sat chatting and drinking. At the end of the evening when the slower music started, I asked nervously if anyone wanted a slow dance with me. I hoped that Dougie might offer to dance with me, but to my surprise Steve, one of his friends, agreed to have a slow dance. Steve was a very quiet young man who was crazy about motorbikes. As we danced, I held him tight and I could sense that both of us were getting aroused.

Over the coming months, when Dougie was out with his fiancée, I invited Steve to my house and he accompanied me to the club a few times. Steve even stayed the night once or twice, but although he shared my bed, he never showed any desire for further sexual contact and I didn't force myself on him. He was a substitute for Dougie, but his looks and character were quite different. I liked him, but I did not feel love for him like I had for Dougie. I taught Steve to drive a car and he taught me to ride a motorbike. I bought him clothes and even bought a motorbike from him, and we used to go for rides with some other friends. I always received a welcome from the parents of both these young men. Although I feel sure they realised that I was gay, they were happy to see me and to offer me tea and cake. They seemed to appreciate the care and attention I had given to their sons and the fact that I had not taken advantage of them. Then a day came when Steve became ill and I had to rush him and his mum in my car to a hospital in London. He had kidney failure and was ill for some time, and finally received a kidney transplant. Meanwhile, Dougie was getting married and, to my surprise, he asked me to be his "Best Man" at his wedding. It wasn't easy for me to take this role, but I accepted and duly gave a little speech at their wedding. As for me, I was lonely and on my own again.

Chapter 8

"A Lover at Last."

I had reached the age of thirty, and longed to settle down with someone. One night I had a dream of myself with a blond haired woman in a car together. It seemed as if we were a couple. I would have liked to have been married with a family, but I couldn't imagine how that could ever happen.

I was still sharing my house with the two other guys. We each had our own different lives, and they tolerated my gay lifestyle. One Saturday night, I was on my own and feeling lonely. I decided to go to the gay club, hoping to meet someone nice, and I got there at around eleven o'clock in the evening. Having bought myself a drink, I stood near the back of the room, looking around. Loud music was playing and the club was crowded. I could see some familiar people standing by the bar or sitting at tables, while others were already dancing to the music. But as I looked around I couldn't see anyone new or interesting. I prepared myself for another lonely, fruitless evening.

After a few minutes, I decided to move nearer to the front, where the DJ was playing the records. I had to step around some people on the edge of the dance-floor, when suddenly I came face-to-face with a little guy in a checked shirt. This wasn't just any checked shirt! It was identical to one that I had bought for Dougie, a couple of years earlier, and that I had loved to see him wearing. Now this guy in front of me was small and boyish, with a short haircut and soft brown eyes. I smiled at him, and he returned a shy smile. I was attracted to him, and I sensed that he liked me too. It was really difficult to have a conversation as we were standing close to one of the large loud-speakers, and he spoke rather quietly. I managed to hear that his name was Jimmy. We danced to some disco records, and tried to have a conversation. After a while, Jimmy apologised and said he had leave now, as he had come with some friends. I asked if he'd like to meet again and he agreed, so we arranged to meet a few days later.

We met again later the next week at his bed-sit. Jimmy seemed kind, and rather timid. We were very different in character and interests, yet we were both tired with one night relationships and lonely living. We seemed to get on together. He told me that he was soon due to spend a few weeks in France, as he had been doing a language course at evening class, as well as a clerical job in the daytime. As my French grandmother was still alive, I had the idea of taking a holiday at the same time in August. After visiting her in Normandy, I could drive to Brittany to meet Jimmy on the day his course was due to finish. Jimmy agreed to this. We were both taking quite a risk! Who was to say that I would show up there, or that he would still want to see me? There were no mobile phones in those days!

August had arrived. Jimmy had already been gone a few weeks and I left home to visit "grandmere", taking my car across on the ferry. After spending a couple of days with her in her little flat, I drove a couple of hundred kilometres west to Brittany. I arrived with time to spare. At the appointed time, I parked and waited in the car near the building where Jimmy said he would be. I said to myself, "Will Jimmy show up? Or will I be left feeling stupid and disappointed?"

People started coming out of the building, and then, there was Jimmy, right on cue. He seemed relieved to see me too. We still had the weekend in front of us before being booked on a return ferry, so we spent two or three days and nights together in Brittany staying wherever we could find some room. It was fun, sexy and quite romantic. At last I had found someone I liked and who seemed to like me, both as a person and in a sexual way. Jimmy was shy and easy to get along with, and a friendship was already growing between us.

After our return from holiday we continued to meet up together. Before long, I asked Jimmy if he would like to move in to my house with me. He said that he would, and that he was happy to change his job and leave Southampton. That autumn, Jimmy moved in to share my house and my bedroom. The other two guys were still renting their rooms, but seemed not to be bothered by Jimmy's arrival as my boy-friend. Jimmy applied for a job in a nearby village as a trainee picture-framer, and was offered the job. I drove him there each morning before going to my office, and he would catch a bus back. We seemed settled together, but then, near the start of our relationship, I nearly caused us to break up.

Jimmy was small in stature and low in self-confidence. He had grown up with two more dominant older sisters, and as a boy he had preferred to hang around with the girls at his school. I liked his gentle character and his looks, but his way of talking and his mannerisms were sometimes rather effeminate. I liked "boyish" boys, and I hurt and embarrassed Jimmy a few times with critical comments in front of other friends. At Christmas-time, Jimmy went home to visit his parents who lived in the Midlands. He was due to be away for a week or more. Meanwhile I spent Christmas at home, visiting my parents and other family members. Shortly after Christmas, I received a letter from Jimmy. In it he said that he really liked me, but that I had hurt him deeply with my critical comments and he didn't know if he could continue in a relationship with me. Tears came to my eyes as I read the letter and realised how proud and selfish I had been. I wrote back immediately, apologising for hurting him and promising to try to stop doing it. He replied straight away, saying he was grateful for my apology and forgave me. So, after New Year 1978, we were back together again as a couple. During this year both other guys moved out to live with their girlfriends and we were left with the house to ourselves. I taught Jimmy to drive, and he passed his driving test first time. I helped him buy an old car with which he could drive to his work and back. We became very bonded to each other, and no longer bothered to visit gay pubs or clubs. We visited his parents who were very kind to me and welcomed me as their son's partner. I also introduced Jimmy to my parents, but their reaction was predictably much less enthusiastic! At last I had a friend who gave back to me love and sexual attraction. We were happy together, spent our leisure time together, and lived together faithfully as a couple.

Yet, despite all this, we both felt that there was something missing in our lives. Jimmy began to investigate Eastern religions, especially Hare Krishna. He read to me out of books he had bought, but I was not so impressed. I remember saying that surely Jesus Christ was supposed to be the way to heaven. I believed in God, but had no relationship with him then. Jimmy persuaded me to accompany him to a Hare Krishna temple in London. It was above a shoe shop in the West End. We had to remove our shoes, and I sat there during some chanting and ringing of bells. The High Priest was there, and he and his followers had shaven heads like Buddhist monks. The High Priest gave a talk, but everything went over my head; I felt like a reporter, listening, but not involved.

At the end of the talk there was an opportunity for questions. To my great surprise, a guy with an Australian accent stood up and accused the High Priest of being a "snake in the grass." This guy had some friends with him and suddenly they became involved in a punch-up, as the shaven-headed peace-loving monks tried to forcibly evict the noisy trouble-makers. The meeting broke up in chaos, and Jimmy and I were glad to get out without being punched or kicked. On the way home, I said to Jimmy; "Well, so much for their peaceful religion!"

Jimmy too was disappointed and disillusioned. The following weekend arrived; Sunday was always a difficult day to fill. On this particular Sunday morning, I heard myself say; "How about we try church this week? There is one just a few minutes' walk away."

We didn't know anything about this church or its' service times, but at 10.30 that Sunday morning, two guys in jeans walked in and sat near the back of a packed church, just as the service was about to start. Jimmy had been a choir-boy as a lad, and I had attended school chapel, so we were used to hymns and prayers. But what I hadn't bargained for was the presence of the Holy Spirit. As we sang a hymn that I knew well, suddenly there it was again; that feeling of supernatural love which I had felt before as a boy. The feeling soon passed, but I enjoyed the experience of church. After that, Jimmy and I returned most Sundays.

During the summer, we took a holiday, driving through Europe. This holiday was enjoyable and romantic, as well as being tiring. We arrived home safely, and there was no heartache of parting company, as I had experienced with Dougie. However, even though our friendship was strong and we loved each other, yet still we both felt somehow incomplete. One Sunday in October 1979, we both went to church as usual. This Sunday morning, the vicar spoke about commitment; particularly about committing every area of your life to Jesus Christ. As he was speaking, I felt a welling-up of emotion inside me. I felt that I might suddenly burst out sobbing. The feeling of love surrounded me and intensified. It was as if I was alone in the church, with only the sound of the vicar's voice in the distance. I found myself saying; "Lord Jesus, I never knew I could commit my life to you!"

I wondered if I had spoken these words aloud. But as the vicar finished speaking, I looked around and no-one was staring at me. During the last hymn I could hardly control the emotion that was welling up inside me. As soon as everyone knelt down for the final blessing, I too knelt down and prayed quietly; "Lord Jesus, forgive me my sins. I commit my life to you."

Something like a dam broke inside! I began to weep and sob, covering my face with my hands. At the same time, a feeling of inner cleansing was taking place. When I composed myself, the church organ was playing and people were starting to leave their seats. No-one seemed to have noticed my sobbing; only Jimmy, who had been sitting next to me. As we walked home, I told him that something had happened to me, though I didn't know quite what it was. Later that day, Jimmy went upstairs by himself and also prayed for Jesus to come into his life. Without any human intervention, two souls had been "born again" that Sunday.

Just a few days later, we received a visit from the vicar. He knew we were new to the congregation and probably guessed that we were a gay couple, but he did not seem to know about our new commitment. We were too shy to say anything to him about it, so we made polite conversation and he left. We had never been visited by a vicar before, and we felt quite honoured by it. We continued going to church, and each of us bought a Bible. After a short time, we were invited to a meal by a family in the church. Again the conversation was general and superficial, but we felt accepted by these people as a couple. I had started to read my Bible, and after reading the gospel stories about Jesus and the exciting miracles in the "Acts of the apostles", I moved on to Paul's letter to the Romans. To my dismay, I read about God's condemnation of homosexual behaviour. At first I felt condemned and rejected. I thought to myself, "How could God accept me now?" Then I remembered the feeling of his deep love surrounding me, even as a child before my sexuality had developed. I realised that he did love me and Jimmy too, so it must be our sexual behaviour that was not what he intended? Jimmy had also felt the same thoughts independently from me. After a short while, we took a difficult and painful step. We decided to live together as a couple, but not share a bedroom or a bed; in other words, not have sexual contact any more. This was easier said than done, and there were times when the need for contact and sexual release overcame us.

One day, we made another trip to see Jimmy's parents. As before, they put us in their spare bedroom, sharing a double bed together. Temptation was too much for us and we hugged and aroused each other. The following morning was a Sunday and we decided to attend a local charismatic church nearby. During the service an elderly man spoke in "tongues". An interpretation was given by another person in English, but I didn't hear much of it. I was sobbing too much! And so was Jimmy! The feeling we received was not like an angry rebuke from a judgemental God. On the contrary, it felt more like the tender comfort of a mother, and a demonstration of deep love and compassion for us both. From this point forwards, Jimmy and I shared our home as best-friends, but without sexual activity together. Of course this was not easy to do, as we still had love and attraction towards each-other.

Chapter 9

"Good and Evil."

I soon became aware of a family who often arrived late at the church for the Sunday morning service. They were a mother and two daughters. They looked out-of-place in this congregation of mostly professional people. The mother looked bedraggled, wearing worn and dirty clothes, and slippers with holes in them. The older daughter was always at the front, leading the way, while the younger one followed her like a sheep follows the shepherd; the mum was at the rear of the group. There were no smiles on their faces. Rather, a look of rejection and pain, and of suspicion towards the other church members. I wondered who they were and why they kept coming week after week. I was bothered by the fact that few in the congregation seemed to take any notice of them, except to avoid sitting too near them, but I realised that this was partly because the mum would usually fall asleep during the sermon, snoring loudly. I decided to approach the mother and ask if she would like some new shoes. I did so the following Sunday. She looked surprised, but said that she would like new shoes. I asked for her shoe size, and the following week I gave her a pair of slip-on shoes. I had not yet spoken to either of her daughters.

The "harvest supper" was drawing near, and the church was planning an evening of music and entertainment to celebrate the season. I had begun to play my guitar again and had written one or two Christian songs, so I asked if I could sing one of these songs during the entertainment. It was agreed, so I asked my brother Andrew if he would play guitar as well. Even though Andrew was not a church-goer, he was happy to do so. The celebration evening arrived, and we performed the song.

The mother and her two daughters had arrived at the church hall just as I was starting to sing. The older daughter looked towards the stage to see who was singing. At that moment, she had a strange experience. She felt as if she had known the man who was singing all her life; as if their spirits were somehow joined together. This impression lasted for only a few seconds and then was gone.

The following Sunday, after the service had finished, I was standing in the church hall, when a person jumped onto my back from behind. I thought it must be one of the children, but to my surprise it was this girl. She had never spoken to me before and this action seemed most unlike her. She told me that her dad was in hospital, dying of cancer, and she was asking people to pray for him. I said that I would pray, and she moved on to ask someone else. The next Sunday she approached me again and said that her dad had died earlier in the week. I felt compassion for this family, and wanted to try to help them. I discovered their address and a few days later I went round with some food and provisions. The older sister answered the door and invited me in. She told me that her name was Maureen, and she introduced me to her sister Sally, and to Johnny, one of her three brothers. She said that her two youngest brothers were at their children's home. Their house was old, cold and dirty, with no central heating. Her mum, whose name was Joan, was also in the room, slumped in an armchair, smoking a cigarette. In front of her was an ashtray filled with cigarette butts, and the house smelt of damp and tobacco smoke. I felt awkward and embarrassed, not knowing what to talk about, but they seemed to appreciate my visit and especially the groceries.

I soon discovered that life for this family had been full of poverty, neglect, abuse, rejection and abandonment. Joan had been rejected at birth by her own mother and had suffered with mental illness for most of her life. She had met George, a man twenty years older than herself. He was an alcoholic, having been traumatised in the army as a young man. Joan and George were never married, but they had five children over a period of six years. Now he had just died.

I started to befriend this family, not really knowing why. I took them on outings and even trips to the sea-side, and acted rather like a father-figure to them. I soon discovered that Maureen, as the oldest child, had been forced to act as "mother" to her mum and her siblings from an early age. Maureen had been sexually abused by several men, and had attempted suicide several times as a teenager. Much of her childhood had been spent in various children's homes, and she had grown up emotionally scarred, distrustful of authority figures and fearful of men. At the age of eighteen, she had asked Jesus into her life, while on bail for petty crime. Days later, she had been committed to the psychiatric wing of Holloway prison, which was a most unpleasant experience. Soon she was placed on probation, and was fostered by a Christian family in Swindon, who had known her as a child. During this time away from her family, she met a couple called Luther and Sandy who were American missionaries, living in England. They befriended her and helped her find part-time work. After nearly a year away from home, she returned to Winchester, to look after her dying father. Her American friend, Sandy, was literally a life-line to her. Sandy faithfully phoned every day after Maureen had returned to Winchester. The family had no telephone at home, so Maureen would have to wait in a callbox down the road for these calls. These conversations and prayerful support helped her to survive during periods of great stress.

Now Maureen and Sally would often walk across town to my house, where Jimmy and I would talk and pray with them. There were times when Maureen was anxious and agitated, overwhelmed by her responsibilities for her family. Sometimes I had no idea how to help her except to be there to listen. Sometimes God would give us words of encouragement through the girls, who had both received the baptism in the Holy Spirit.

Meanwhile, Maureen's brother Johnny had been convicted by the Court for participating in a crime. He had been sentenced to "borstal", a prison for young offenders. It was situated about fifty miles away. The family could not afford to travel this distance by train, so I used the company's minibus a few times to take them to visit Johnny. He appreciated our visits, as otherwise he might not have seen any family members.

Out of the blue one day, I received a telephone call. It was Paul's mother. I had not spoken to her for many years, and fifteen years had now passed since Paul and I first met. His mother sounded agitated and embarrassed, saying that she needed to ask me for a big favour. She explained briefly that in his quest for excitement, Paul had broken off his engagement and had left England to take a job in Papua New Guinea. One of his passions was hand-gliding, and he had been injured in an accident in that country. She said that he had now returned to her house near Winchester, but that he was mentally unwell. In the last day or two, he had tried to commit suicide by taking an overdose of pills. She begged me to take him into my house for a little while. She thought that he might respond better to me as an old friend. Jimmy and I agreed to have him stay a while, not knowing what to expect.

When Paul arrived, I was shocked by his appearance. He looked much older, with bedraggled hair and beard, and he had a strange look in his eyes. The attraction I used to feel towards him was no longer there, but a compassion for him replaced it. He brought with him a strange wooden object with carvings on it. I knew little about witchcraft or voodoo, but I could sense that this object was connected to some sinister evil. During the short time that Paul was in my house, I tried to speak to him about

47

Jesus, and I sang some simple worship songs to him with my guitar. Whenever I did this, I would see his eyes turn red and a look of hatred appear in them. I was a little scared, but he did not try to attack me. I learned that in the hospital in Papua, they have both medical staff and witchdoctors. I knew instinctively that something evil had happened to Paul, but I had no idea how to help him. On Sunday, to my surprise, he agreed to come to church. He stayed very quiet during the service and could not participate, but afterwards I felt an urge to buy him a Bible from the church bookshop. When we returned to my house, I gave him this Bible as a gift.

That Sunday afternoon, I had agreed to take Maureen and her family to visit Johnny in borstal, and the round trip would take all afternoon. I offered for Paul to come with us in the minibus, but he wanted to stay behind. So we left Paul at home, but he did have a small car which he had parked in my garage, situated underneath the biggest bedroom. Paul seemed very quiet, but as I was leaving to collect the others, I noticed that he had picked up the Bible and was looking through its' pages. I felt encouraged by this and said we would see him later, on our return.

I completed the long trip to see Johnny and arrived home after dark with Maureen and her two youngest brothers still with me. We entered the house but there was no sign of Paul. After calling his name with no response, one of us went upstairs to look in his bedroom. There was still no sign of him. I said I would see if his car had gone. I went through the back door leading to the garage, with young Richard following me. I switched on the garage light, and saw that the car was still there. Then I noticed that the windows looked dull and black, and I noticed a piece of garden hose-pipe attached to the exhaust-pipe and leading into a slightly open car window. Fear gripped me. I asked Richard to run back and get Maureen. Meanwhile I tried to open the front door of the car. Inside I found Paul, slumped over the steering wheel. He was dead.

Maureen arrived in the garage and bravely tried to give mouth-to-mouth resuscitation, but it was far too late. In shock, we called for an ambulance. It arrived quickly, but they confirmed that Paul had been dead for some time. There were questions to be answered, and then they took Paul's body away. I wanted to be alone with God for a few moments, so I asked Maureen to make a drink for herself and her brothers. I went up to the bathroom, and knelt down on the floor next to the bath, with my head in my hands, and I cried out to God: "Lord, I have failed you!" I said. "Please forgive me. I left him to die. I didn't know he was going to do that today!"

At that very moment, the presence of the Holy Spirit came into the room and over me, and I heard the most beautiful music, as if from a far-away land. Then a gentle voice spoke clearly into my heart. "Fear not," said the voice, "I am pleased with you. It is not your fault. Satan wanted to have him, but I have rescued him in answer to your prayers. Paul is now here with me." A supernatural peace descended over me which stayed with me for several days. I was able to comfort the others and take them home. The Police had been notified, and later Paul's mother was on the phone to me in a state of shame and guilt. She felt it was all her fault. I comforted her as best I could, and assured her that Paul was now in a much better place. Over the following few days there were further questions and an inquest for me to attend. All through this time I felt that supernatural peace with me. Eventually, Paul's brother came to take away the car from my garage. He also took the wooden carved object to pass on to his mother. I had tried to persuade her to let me destroy it, but she insisted on keeping it.

Chapter 10

"Prophetic Confirmation."

Christmas 1981 had come and gone. By now, Jimmy had also met a Christian girl while working in the picture-framing shop, and they would sometimes see each other outside of working hours. This gave Maureen and I more time to spend together too. We would watch TV, or talk and pray together. I spent many hours trying to help her with her problems, though not with great wisdom or skill. Yet she appreciated having someone who would care about her and her life, as she had been used and abused by so many. Following her dad's death, the council offered the family a change of house, and I helped her mum and family move their few belongings. Their new home was smaller, and had central heating. It was better than the previous cold damp house.

One evening in February, I was taking Maureen back to this house. I parked the car and offered to pray for her before she went in. We prayed for a minute or two, and then instead of getting out of the car, Maureen sat still and asked me, "Is Jesus saying anything to you?" I had to admit that I didn't get to hear him much at that time.

"I feel that he wants us to take a step of faith together," she said. At first I didn't get it; I wondered what she meant. She had never told me about her supernatural experience at the harvest celebration. Yet God had been hinting at us about plans that he had for us together, but I hadn't really caught on. Then the penny dropped! I sat in silence for a short while before answering her question. "Do you think he means that we should get married?" I asked nervously. "Yes, I think that's what God is saying," she replied quietly. I paused again for a few moments in silence. Thoughts were racing through my brain. I was fond of Maureen and respected her character, but I didn't love her in a romantic or sexual way, though she was an attractive girl. "Could I really marry her?" I asked myself; "Was it fair to her?" Yet in my heart, I wanted to obey God. After a brief silence, I opened my mouth to speak; "OK, let's do it." I heard myself say. "We'll go to town tomorrow and choose an engagement ring."

I know this is not the way most courting couples get engaged! But the following morning, I came round to collect Maureen from her house. But first of all, we wanted to honour a promise we had made to an elderly Pentecostal man who was no longer able to get out and about. He was suffering from arthritic pain and we had offered to call by to pray with him. We arrived at his house and after a brief conversation we began to pray for him for relief from his pain. I had scarcely prayed more than a few words before he started to speak in a loud voice. I stopped praying immediately, thinking that he was rudely interrupting my prayer for him. Then it dawned on me that God was speaking a prophetic word through him to Maureen and I. "You will grow in strength from one another," I heard him say. "There will be much opposition, but I am with you." With these and other words describing the call of God on our lives as a couple, he completed the prophetic word.

I was stunned and amazed! This old man had no idea that we were about to go into town to buy an engagement ring. Now Maureen and I had received prophetic confirmation from God that we were to be married. We shared this with the old man and he was greatly encouraged. Later that morning, we visited a jewellers shop and chose a ring together. Later we began to share our news with family and friends. We experienced some positive and faith-filled reactions to our news and some much more negative ones too.

51

Two months later, Maureen and I had booked to go to a Christian event called "Spring Harvest." It was a long distance away in North Wales and on the morning of our departure I had a migraine headache. We managed to make the journey, but when we arrived at our guest-house, we were tired and weary. We discovered that our room contained a double bed. We had never shared a bed and didn't feel right about doing so now, but all the other rooms were taken. After an evening meal we both tried to settle down to sleep. As soon as we turned off the light, we became aware of an evil presence at the end of the bed. I turned the light back on but still a feeling of coldness remained, and I found myself shaking and shivering.

"Go away in the name of Jesus!" I was saying, but I knew I was fearful inside, and the presence remained. It stayed there all night until daybreak. By now we were exhausted, having been awake all night. Then God worked a miracle for us. In the morning, two people who had booked for the weekend suddenly decided to leave. The manageress offered us their room instead. It had two single beds. We moved rooms and were not troubled again by the evil presence.

After a shaky start, we enjoyed the conference and were blessed. I had prayed that I would receive the baptism of the Holy Spirit there and be able to speak in tongues. But though I tried hard to receive this gift, I had to go home disappointed. However, a few weeks later, Maureen and I were due to visit Luther and Sandy near Swindon. Whilst with them, they took us for a drive in their camper-van. The roads were hilly with a lot of bends, and by the time we reached their planned destination, I was feeling unwell with travel sickness and another migraine headache. I wanted to take a walk in the fresh air. But, to my horror, they suggested that this was the time to receive the gift I wanted! I had no strength to argue as I was feeling quite ill. They began to pray for me and one little foreign-sounding word came to my lips. I spoke it out aloud.

"That's it!" said Sandy, "you've received the baptism; that's the start!" No more words came that day, but over the following week a few more words were added. Yet, when I prayed in tongues, I would always say the same six or seven words over and over. One evening, Maureen offered to pray with me for a greater release of this gift. I wasn't trying so hard in my own strength any more, and suddenly as I spoke my few words, a new language started to flow freely from my mouth. I felt joy and peace. Now I really had received the gift of tongues and I would continue to use it.

Over the coming weeks and months, Maureen and I had time to plan our wedding, including the hymns and songs for the service itself. We had asked Luther to be "Best Man", and Sandy to sing two songs. They had gladly agreed. Meanwhile, as predicted, we encountered opposition and criticism from certain people within the church, as well as from some members of my family.

Chapter 11

"Wedding Vows."

The date was March 26th 1983. I had reached the age of 36, just five days earlier. My young bride, Maureen, was still only 22. Our wedding day had arrived.

There had been opposition to our marriage, just as God had foretold. Within my family there was concern over my ability to be a husband, and even suspicion over Maureen's motives for marrying me. My family had by now acquired a degree of status and wealth in the local community, while Maureen's family were without money or status, living in a council house in a deprived part of town. Even the church congregation had been split in opinion by our engagement. There were members of the congregation who showed us support and encouragement, believing that God was directing us and would bless us. But there were others who showed coldness of heart and rejection, especially towards Maureen. Some even accused her openly of "gold-digging", and manipulation towards me. For someone already so broken by rejection and pain in her childhood, this was deeply hurtful to her. As for me, I know that some church members were aware of my sexuality and my former relationship with Jimmy, but very few seemed to take notice of it. There was one dear man who took Jimmy and I under his wing in the early days and sought to counsel us. We joined his home-group and he spent time with us. Luther and Sandy also spent time with us both in prayer and counselling, by phone and by personal visit. Finally, our new vicar also saw me once a week for prayer and support. Apart from these people, the subject of sexuality was never really mentioned.

Meanwhile, Maureen and I pressed through with our wedding plans, sensing a peace and the Father's protective hand over us. Many encouragements came our way as we prepared for the wedding day. The new Vicar gave us both marriage preparation advice, and he was positive about conducting our marriage service with his blessing. He even offered the normally chargeable parts of the service for free, including the use of the church hall for the wedding reception. We received other offers of help from some church members too. One lady made a beautiful three-tier wedding cake; another made bridesmaid dresses from material that we had chosen; others supplied and prepared buffet-style food for the reception and a gentleman offered his car and himself as chauffeur to bring Maureen to the church on the wedding day.

We ourselves bought a wedding outfit with shoes and hat for Maureen's mum, as she had no money, and nothing suitable to wear. I also lent three of my office suits to Maureen's three brothers. But what would Maureen herself wear? Wedding dresses were very expensive. To our amazement, a neighbour who we only knew casually, heard about our engagement and offered Maureen the use of a dress which she had worn twenty years earlier for her own wedding. This dress had been hand-made and was beautiful, and it fitted Maureen perfectly. We felt that God was saying that as you bless others, he will bless you even more. Finally, a few weeks before the wedding, Jimmy announced that he too had become engaged to the Christian girl from his workplace, and they would be married later that year.

So the day of our marriage arrived! Luther was "Best Man," and Sandy sang her two songs beautifully. Maureen's oldest brother Johnny was now back home and he took the role of "Father of the Bride". All the members of my family and of her family were there, together with Jimmy, his fiancée and members of his family. Most of my friends who had known me before I was a Christian were also present, including Dougie with his new wife and his mum and family; also Steve and his parents, and my former house-sharers. There were also a good number from the church congregation at the service.

In the sermon the vicar spoke about the wedding at Cana in Galilee where Jesus performed his first miracle, turning jugs of water into fine wine. Both Maureen and I were surprisingly peaceful throughout the service and when we went to the altar for the last hymn, I sensed that wonderful loving presence of God around me, and briefly lifted up my hands to him in thanks and praise. I believe I heard him say; "Well done, my dear children. You have obeyed my call and have overcome opposition. I have blessed you both on your wedding day."

Having signed the register, we came out of the church together as man and wife. There followed a series of wedding photographs, with my brother Andrew acting as wedding photographer. Then we joined the reception in the church hall and mingled amongst the guests who were enjoying the buffet food. We were both too excited and occupied to eat much. The afternoon seemed to fly by. Soon the time came for us to change into more casual clothes and leave by car for our honeymoon destination. After saying thanks and goodbye, we drove out of the church driveway with friends and relatives waving us off. We both felt very happy about how everything had worked out, but also very drained by all the attention we had received. We had booked a night in a hotel about an hour's drive away for the first night of our honeymoon. By the time we arrived at this hotel we were both feeling tired after all the excitement, but a meal in the restaurant revived us.

I began to feel anxious about our first night sleeping together as a couple. In my mind I felt pressure and expectation to "perform" sexually as a man. Up to this point in our relationship, Maureen and I had done little more than holding hands. As we prepared to share a bed together I felt tense and embarrassed. After the earlier sense of blessing, I now felt a threat of failure, as I realised that the chemistry of romantic love and sexual attraction was missing, at least for me, in our relationship. Soon we were in the bedroom and preparing for bed. I felt shy and embarrassed to undress in front of my new wife. Worse still, as I tried to make love to her, the memories of earlier sexual encounters with girls surfaced in my thoughts, and some feelings of revulsion towards women came into my mind. I felt unable to explain these things to Maureen and after a few minutes of attempted love-making, I finished up frustrated and tearful, feeling useless and a failure as a husband. Somehow I had imagined that God would instantly transform my sexuality on our wedding night, simply because I had obeyed his call to marriage. I was to discover that the changes in me were to take place over many years and would involve him changing much more than just my sexuality! I was also to discover that Maureen herself had experienced feelings of fear and dread on that first night together, as memories of childhood sexual abuse were triggered in her mind. For her too, it would take many years to be changed and healed. Our marriage could not be based simply on lust or sexual attraction. We would have to love one another as close friends and companions, allowing God to bring change and even romance into our marriage as he worked his healing in us.

The following day we returned to my house in Winchester. I had used all my savings to book a trip to Israel as our main honeymoon, where we would visit the Holy Land. We were to join a party from a church a few miles away. We had allowed ourselves a day or two at home to relax after the wedding, before making the journey. Jimmy had moved out of my house a few days before the wedding and had been offered accommodation by a Christian couple from our church. He drove us to Heathrow airport. Maureen had never flown in a plane before, so it was something of a nerve-racking experience for her and I too was nervous of flying at that time.

Once we were safely arrived and had gone through customs and out to our waiting coach, we were accosted and followed by a crowd of boys and young Arab men begging tourists for money. Maureen was overcome by emotions of panic, finding herself far from home in a strange environment, and she started begging me to take her home. Of course, I could not, so I tried to comfort her as best I could. In the end we were blessed by our ten days in the land where Jesus walked, talked and did miracles. We found some difficulties in joining in with group activities, but we did go on some of the sight-seeing outings. We particularly enjoyed sitting and praying together at the "Garden Tomb" in Jerusalem, and in some of the quieter locations in Galilee. The trip gave us an opportunity to spend time together far away from our usual location and to learn how to care about and be considerate to one-another. After ten days in Israel, we flew back to Heathrow, where Jimmy collected us and drove us home. Now the time had come for us to settle into married life together.

I returned to my job with the family business while Maureen looked after the house. I had already joined a group of Christian businessmen who met regularly for prayer and fellowship. The organisation was called the "Full Gospel Businessmen's Fellowship International", or FGBMFI for short. Jimmy and I had been part of the local Winchester chapter which arranged outreach dinners with a Christian speaker once every month. Maureen had come with me to several of these dinners, and we had invited her brothers and other friends too. A fortnight or so after our return from Israel we were due to attend a local FGBMFI dinner. There was a pleasant meal, worship and singing, good fellowship and an excellent and humorous speaker. We arrived home late, feeling relaxed and blessed. As we prepared to turn in for the night, to my surprise, we had our first time of sexual intimacy together. Our earlier difficulties were still apparent, but were less intrusive. Within a week or two, Maureen started to feel some symptoms of sickness, and very soon a test confirmed that she was pregnant. We now understood why God helped us to be intimate after that dinner and that he had plans for us to have a child sooner than we expected. We decided to ask him in prayer for a suitable name for the child, and to our surprise, we both received two names into our thoughts. The names were David and Esther. One was a King and the other a Queen in Old Testament times. We had read about praying blessing upon the child in the womb by laying-on of hands, so we tried to do this regularly. I imagined that because of my past background, God would not give us a boy first, but when the time for giving birth drew near, Maureen became convinced that the baby was a boy.

Chapter 12

"Pain and Testing."

My health was gradually deteriorating. I was going to work each day to the family business, but I would become tired and weary, and would have to return home at lunchtime for a rest. As winter approached the symptoms grew worse and it became necessary to rest for longer periods. Eventually I was only able to work a very few hours each day. I consulted a doctor and was given sedatives, but nothing seemed to help. Christmas arrived, and the baby was due in January. On the day after Christmas, Pop telephoned and asked me to come to his house to see him. When I arrived, I noticed that my step-mother looked sad, as if she had been crying. My father called me into his dining room. His face looked grave. "I am going to have to release you from the family business" he stated, "as you are no longer able to do your job properly. I have decided to let you keep your company car."

I don't remember much else as the shock of being dismissed from the family business left me stunned and speechless. I arrived home to break the news to Maureen and she too felt shocked and rejected. I was about to enter parenthood with a nervous illness and no job. We tried to pray for help and guidance but were still too anxious to hear from God. Within just a few days Maureen began to have labour pains. We made one trip to the maternity unit which came to nothing, but a day or so later labour pains began in earnest and Maureen was admitted into the labour ward under the care of a midwife from our church.

Once again my dreams and expectations were about to be challenged! Having been given the names of our children by God, I imagined that these kids would be like little angels, coming into this world with great joy and peace and growing up close to God right from early childhood. But as the labour pains continued hour after hour and Maureen became increasingly distressed, fear and anxiety began to grip me. After spending a few hours at the hospital I went home to try to rest for a while, but it was impossible to relax. In the middle of the night I received a call from the hospital asking me to return as soon as possible. When I arrived I found Maureen struggling in a state of near-exhaustion. She had been in labour for more than twenty-four hours and she was weak and frightened.

The senior midwife had been determined to deliver the child herself. But now a state of panic began to take hold of the situation, as it became clear that the baby's head was turned sideways and had become stuck fast, still high up in the birth canal. This was a very dangerous situation as Maureen's strength was failing and the baby's life was now in grave danger. An urgent call was made for an off-duty doctor to attend as soon as possible. Minutes later a slightly-built Oriental man hurried into the room to assess the situation. He was visibly shocked by what he found, and reprimanded the midwife for not calling him much earlier. He had been on duty at the hospital earlier that evening, but now had been called in from his home to an emergency. He made a rapid appraisal of the situation. "It is far too late for a Caesarian section!" he said abruptly. "This baby has only minutes to live. I am going to have to use high forceps!"

I assisted the nurses in holding Maureen's arms as firmly as we could while the doctor performed a dangerous and painful procedure. He inserted the long forceps to the place where the baby's head was stuck, gripping either side of the head with them. Then, using all his strength, he made a twisting motion to free the baby's head; this was followed by a strong tugging motion. As the nurses and I held onto Maureen, the doctor pulled the baby out of the birth canal by force. This was extremely unpleasant for Maureen. She felt as if she was having her womb pulled out of her body. Thankfully, both she and the baby were still alive.

"It's a boy!" exclaimed one of the nurses, as the baby let out a weak cry. They tried to place him on Maureen's chest but she was too shocked and exhausted to react. A nurse took the baby to one side to be cleaned up and placed him in a glass-topped cot. The baby, also in deep shock, lay there motionless with his eyes staring at the bright lights. I looked down at him and said softly, "Hello David, I'm Daddy." I too was still in a state of shock.

Maureen had to have several stitches followed by a chance to rest. Later, they gave David to her and she tried to breast-feed him, but without success. I returned home and began to contact close family and friends to give them the news, and later my step-mother and then the vicar came to visit her. Both seemed surprised at how exhausted Maureen looked and the vicar prayed for rest and peace. She was later prescribed medication to calm her nerves and help her sleep.

By the following day David was still not taking milk, even from a bottle. Suddenly Maureen noticed his face and body turning blue and she called out urgently for help. Fortunately there was an experienced middle-aged nurse passing close by. She took one look and snatched David from Maureen's arms and hurried to a nearby room, telling Maureen to stay where she was and not to try to follow. But Maureen, still weak and in pain from the stitches, managed to shuffle towards the room where the nurse in her haste, had left the door slightly ajar. Without entering the room, Maureen saw her putting a tube down the baby's throat and sucking something from his lungs. For the second time in as many days, baby David had been close to death, but God preserved his life. After this incident David was then able to take milk from a bottle and he and Maureen began to recover from their ordeal.

After another day or two in hospital, Maureen was desperate to come home with the baby. She had a fear of hospitals dating right back to an accident when she was only three years old. Now she was finding difficulty in resting and sleeping, so the doctors decided to let her go home with David to recover. Once she was home, I was able to help her with domestic duties, food-shopping, cooking, etc., as well as some nappy changing and bottle feeding. During the first few weeks Maureen was still quite weak, so my help around the house was useful to her. We quickly discovered that David had a great fear of being left alone and of falling asleep. One of us had to be near him all the time and he would scream if left alone in a room, even for just a few moments. At bed-time he would cry and become distressed and he could not fall asleep unless someone was there to rub his back and comfort him. Maureen and I could often be seen walking the streets after dark with a baby in a pram or a pushchair, trying to send him to sleep. Over the course of time this problem seemed to get worse and not better. Some friends told us to leave him to scream, but we couldn't bear to see how distressed he became. We asked the doctor for advice and he gave us a medicine to make him drowsy at night, but even this had little effect. So we continued back-rubbing, reading stories, singing songs, and praying for him. Most of this was my job over many years of childhood.

After a year on unemployment benefit I was offered a position on a community work program. This was a paid job in the offices of the local County Council. The work was of a clerical nature and quite simple and without stress. It was due to last for just twelve months, but in the end the time period was extended by a few extra months. During this time Maureen and I were able to enjoy some recovery of health, and although my job was rather monotonous, at least I was working, earning a wage and regaining some self-worth.

We attended church regularly and still participated in the FGBMFI, and we felt we were coping better with life. David had turned one year old and was already walking and starting to say a few words, and he seemed to be an intelligent and active toddler. He smiled easily at adults which endeared him to some of the ladies at the church.

In the late spring of 1985, Maureen became pregnant again. Once again we prayed over the baby in the womb, and this time we felt fairly certain that it would be a girl. Maureen did experience fear and anxiety at times during the pregnancy, especially fear of losing the baby. But she received prayer and was given assurance from God that both she and the baby would be fine. With a boisterous toddler to look after, Maureen was well occupied during this time, and in January 1986, just two weeks after David's second birthday, Maureen was once again admitted to the maternity unit. This time the labour was much quicker and without trauma. Soon I had the wonderful experience of witnessing a normal birth; first the baby's head; then arms, body and legs, all perfectly formed inside the womb. Baby Esther had arrived into the world. This time Maureen was able to hold her to her chest for a few moments, and soon I too was able to hold her in my arms and tell her that I was her Daddy. There was no need for stitches, so Maureen and Esther were soon able to return home. Little David was fascinated by his baby sister. Fortunately Esther was a very placid baby and had no problems with sleeping during those early days.

We continued to live as a family in the house which had been my bachelor-pad. My job had come to an end but I had registered with an agency, who supplied me with clerical jobs.

Meanwhile, Maureen was fully occupied looking after the children and the home.

Chapter 13

"Dark Clouds Gathering."

Although we were managing quite well as a family, Maureen was finding church attendance a struggle, as some people still continued to show suspicion towards her. Her many years of rejection and ill-treatment as a child were often reflected in her reactions to other people. She found it easy to trust in the "Jesus of the Bible", but she couldn't see God in the same light. To her, God appeared distant, angry and unapproachable. The idea of a tender, loving heavenly father was completely alien to her experience, and like so many other broken people, she sub-consciously projected her relationship with her earthly father onto Father God.

Although my experience of an earthly father was also far from perfect, I seemed more able to fit in at church and receive from God during worship. I loved to sense his love and presence. Yet deep-down, the sense of failure and guilt which I carried from childhood, still haunted me. I was conscious of the fact that I was still attracted to boys and young men, even though I no longer acted-out with other men. I felt that I was unable to love and cherish Maureen in the way that I thought other husbands loved their wives. Similarly, she could not show me the physical and emotional warmth that I needed. We resembled a father and daughter in our relationship together. My emotions were rather like a wave in the sea, tossed from one side to another. Sometimes I felt blessed by God, but at other times I was anxious and depressed. I did not doubt my calling from God, but I felt unworthy and unable to live the way I felt he would want; in short, I doubted my ability to follow and obey him.

As my fortieth birthday approached, my state of health was deteriorating. The feelings of anxiety and despair, so troublesome during my twenties, were now troubling me again. I went to a doctor and was given tranquilisers and sleeping pills, but these just made me feel dazed. The anxiety symptoms persisted, yet I managed to hide behind a false smile at church or in public. I appeared to be "O.K." to people outside my family, while inside I was falling apart. I had been offered a job working for a man who was a member of the church and the FGBMFI, doing accounting work for his shop. But it was becoming increasingly difficult for me to function properly. I found decision-making almost impossible and any stress crippling.

In desperation we booked the family on a trip to Grenoble in France, where the FGBMFI were holding their annual conference. It was a beautiful location and there would be speakers and delegates there from many countries. Surely the power of God would be manifested in these meetings? So Maureen and I hoped and prayed that God would do a miracle of healing in me. We arrived in Grenoble and I tried to attend as many meetings as I could manage. Fortunately I could still speak French and could understand the talks which were given in French. But while I received reassurance about my beliefs, still my mental state was unchanged. I had also lost a lot of weight, and struggled to eat properly, so I was looking thin and gaunt. Maureen did her best to care for and amuse the children, but she too was struggling with tiredness and anxiety about me, as well as being far from home in a foreign country.

By the end of the conference we were both very tired and I was no better. As the delegates were starting to leave, Maureen plucked up courage to approach a black African man who was standing near her, to ask him for help. She explained that I was sick with symptoms of anxiety. He quickly gathered a group of African men around us and they began to praise God and pray loudly in tongues. Then some of these men took turns to speak words of prophesy over both myself and young David, laying hands on each of us. I longed to sense the presence of God which I had known before, yet I remained unmoved by God's Spirit and the prophetic words seemed to vanish into thin air.

We were booked to stay one more night at our hotel, but a French couple from the conference insisted that they take us by car to a Christian house of prayer and retreat. We agreed, even though it seemed overwhelming for us, but we wanted to obey God. It seemed a long journey and I felt apprehensive about getting to the airport the next day. On arrival, the people there welcomed us and treated us and the children very kindly. We were given food and afterwards they offered us prayer in French, which only I could understand. Once more my mind and body were so exhausted that I could not receive from God. The next morning a lady took us in her car to a train station, bought us tickets, and put us on a train to the airport. Later that day we flew back to London Heathrow where I had left the car. Somehow, dazed and exhausted, I managed to drive us all safely home.

I managed to have a little rest and sleep over the next day or two, and went again to see the same doctor. He prescribed still more of the same medications. I tried to resume my job at the shop. The owner had been praying that I would be much improved, but he could see that I looked pale and drawn. He even prayed for me himself once or twice in his shop; I did experience some peace briefly, but very soon the symptoms returned. I was becoming distant and short-tempered with the children, and they in turn, were becoming disturbed and fearful of me, with my sudden outbursts of anger and shouting.

I had developed a throbbing sensation from the pulse in my neck which prevented me from falling asleep. After a few nights without sleep, I struggled to walk to work and back. I tried to pray and call on God for help, but nothing seemed to happen. Soon my employer told me not to come in to work anymore but to stay at home and try to rest. I took to my bed and shut myself away, even from my family. Yet still I could not sleep or rest properly. I felt tormented and desperate. I began to have thoughts of suicide but felt that Maureen and the children needed me and would not survive without me. I even talked to her about driving us all in the car at high speed over a cliff or into a motorway bridge. Maureen was becoming increasingly frightened and was trying to get help for me from other Christians, but nobody seemed to know how to help. After thirteen days and nights without sleep, she took me to see our vicar. He was very concerned but felt that it was a mainly spiritual problem. He suggested that we try to find an hour together to offer a sacrifice of thanks and praise to God. So that evening, we struggled to get the children to bed as they too were being badly affected by the atmosphere in our home. Eventually they were both asleep together in our large spare-room over the garage. I took hold of my guitar and we tried to sing praises to God. Our efforts seemed pathetic and after trying to sing a few songs, nothing had happened. There was no sudden breakthrough. I felt exhausted, discouraged and desperate.

Suddenly, something like a dark cloud spread over me, and powerful thoughts of suicide came into my head. I stood up trembling. I went to the kitchen drawer and grabbed a carving knife in my hand. Maureen fell to her knees on the floor and pleaded with me not to kill myself. I put the knife down and went to my bedroom with my head thumping. She left me alone and went into the big bedroom with the children. As I lay on the bed, I reached out to take a piece of paper and a pen. I wrote a letter to Maureen saying that I could not go on living like this any longer, and that I wanted to die. After doing so, I sensed an evil presence coming into my bedroom. I saw the curtains flap, even though the window was shut, and felt a chilling presence, but could see no-one. Then a sinister and mocking voice seemed to speak aloud into my soul. The voice said chillingly; "Now you have utterly failed in life in every way. You can no longer call yourself a Christian; now you belong to Satan!"

The voice continued to speak, telling me to expect terrible things to happen and that I was destined for hell with no hope of escape or redemption. At the same time, I felt a shuddering sensation inside my body and wondered if I was now filled with demons. My despair was now fuelled with even greater feelings of fear and hopelessness. I had believed these words and now, beyond death, there was nothing for me but hell itself.

I left my room during the night and walked the streets in despair. Maureen found my suicidal letter the next morning and ran to the curate's house. He came over, closely followed by the vicar, and at the same moment I returned to the house in a state of fear and exhaustion. The vicar wanted to admit me to a Christian retreat house, but I refused, saying that it was too late for me now. They contacted my father who agreed to take me to his house to "recuperate", but I was no better there. I wanted to escape from everything, but I had nowhere to go to escape from the fear and torment.

The following day, Maureen arranged for someone to drive me to Luther and Sandy's home about sixty miles away, to receive some deliverance ministry. I had to escape from my parent's house and be picked up outside in the road. But once at their home, after talking with me, they concluded that my mental condition was beyond this type of ministry. I was brought back to my own house to see my family once more. Soon Pop arrived at our home accompanied by a different doctor from the practice. This doctor looked extremely concerned about me and after asking me some questions, he announced that a place had already been arranged for me in a psychiatric hospital at Marchwood, near Southampton. Maureen hurriedly packed a few of my things in a bag and Pop took me in his car to the hospital. I was silent on the thirty minute journey. Although I knew where I was and could see where we were going, yet another part of my brain believed that I was already dead. When we arrived at the hospital I was laid down on a bed and wheeled into the hallway of a large building. I thought I was being wheeled into a mortuary!

A powerful medication was given to me, which sent me to sleep for the first time in over two weeks. When I awoke, I was in a room lying on a bed. There was a nurse sitting in the corner of the room. I realised that I was alive, but I was still full of fear. After a day or so, having had questions from nurses and doctors, I was allowed to leave the room and walk about. If I went outside, there would always with someone following me in case I tried to run away or kill myself. But I didn't want to die anymore because I was convinced that a worse hell was awaiting me after death. I could not eat because of my state of fear and when a psychiatrist interviewed me, I kept repeating that I had failed as a Christian and was going to hell. They couldn't understand my spiritual condition and classified me as suffering from "Religious Mania." I was heavily medicated, and as days went by I managed to eat a little food, but I was haunted by thoughts that I would become a terrible person and commit all sorts of crimes and abuse to others.

It was compulsory at this hospital for the patients to attend occupational therapy sessions as part of their treatment. These were often in the shape of simple quizzes or games, and I tried to join in as best I could. But one morning we were placed at tables, each with a sheet of paper and colouring crayons. The therapist asked each of us to try to draw a picture depicting our lives to the present point of time and beyond into the future, if

71

we could imagine that. I drew a winding road, and on it I noted down some of the good and bad things that had happened along the way. But when I came to the present time, the road ended abruptly and I drew a cloud of total blackness where the road ended. There was no future for me at all beyond this point.

This drawing must have rung alarm bells with the staff, as soon afterwards I was given electric shock treatment to the brain. This treatment was repeated again on two subsequent occasions, the purpose being to erase bad memories and shock the brain into more positive activity. But the root of my fear could not be removed by this treatment, so little difference was noted. My wife and my family were given a very poor prognosis for my recovery. They were told that I would probably have to remain heavily medicated for the rest of my life and that I would not be able to work again. At this point, both my father and the vicar were forced to conclude that I could not cope with having a wife and children, and that I should return to my old way of life, if ever I was well enough to do so.

My father called Maureen to his house and gave her this prognosis; he offered her a sum of money and a small house for her and the children, if she would agree to divorce me and never see me again. Maureen was stunned, yet boldly replied that she had married me for better or for worse and that this proposed action would finally finish me off. My father said that he admired her loyalty but the offer was there if she ever changed her mind.

Chapter 14

"Glimmers of Light."

I was allowed home for Christmas, still heavily medicated and fearful. I kept saying that I was bad and repeating this over and over again. I was told not to keep saying this; that I was really a good person, but hearing this from other people made no difference. I had believed the lies sown into my soul as a child, and the lies spoken to me by demonic forces. I stayed at home for about three months but the root of my fear was still untouched. I was still hiding away from people and struggling to relate to Maureen and the kids. By the spring, my condition was not improving and I was once again admitted to Marchwood hospital.

The surroundings there were familiar to me, and though I was still fearful and depressed, a nurse was not assigned to follow me around as before. Maureen was sad to see me go into hospital again, but there was no shock or panic this time, and she continued to seek advice and help for me in my absence. She heard of a Christian ministry who were seeking to help and encourage men from a homosexual background who had become Christians. She spoke to them by phone and she found them to be compassionate and sympathetic. They offered one of their members, living in the area, to visit me in hospital. Maureen came to visit me and told me about this offer. Even though I still believed that there was no way back for me, I agreed to meet this visitor.

A few days later a young man called Peter came to visit me. To my surprise, he turned out to be the younger brother of Phil, a man I knew through the FGBMFI. Peter told me that he was gay, yet he spoke positively about his faith in Jesus. He told me that he knew of other gay men who had experienced despair and thoughts of suicide. He said that he could tell from talking to me that I still wanted to believe in Jesus, but that the devil had deceived me into believing there was no hope for me. He said that there were various meetings and conferences taking place these days to encourage men and women with all kinds of sexual brokenness to receive acceptance and belonging in the church and the forgiving love of God. He said that Jesus had promised never to leave us or forsake us. I listened intently to these words. But I still needed to believe all this by personal experience. Yet Peter's words began to spark a glimmer of hope in my soul.

Meanwhile, Andrew also visited me regularly at the hospital and usually brought Maureen and the children with him. He and his wife had been very helpful to my family during both periods in hospital. They had offered them meals and outings, as well as lifts to the hospital. Andrew had been shocked and angry when I was dismissed from the family business, and blamed my father for my breakdown. Pop and my step-mother also visited me several times in hospital. On this second admission they were allowed to take me outside the hospital grounds for a meal. One day, after taking me for lunch in a local pub, we returned to the hospital. Pop then said to me:

"Bruce, I believe that I am 70% responsible for your breakdown. I have been too harsh with you in the past. I never understood you very well, and I'm very sorry."

These words touched something deep inside of me. I had always felt such a disappointment to my father and he had never apologised before for the harsh words he had spoken to me. Although I displayed little emotional reaction outwardly to his apology, inside I felt that something which had been broken was being repaired. I felt that another glimmer of hope had been ignited in my soul.

I did not receive any further electric shock treatment this time, but a psychiatrist decided to start me on lithium, which acts as a mood stabiliser and is used to treat a chemical imbalance in the brain. It takes a little time to be fully effective, but I began to look less tormented and to eat better. After two or three more weeks had passed, I was considered ready to be sent home once again.

Pop came to fetch me in his car. It was a stormy day with dark clouds and rain, but as we drove away from the hospital the sun came shining through and a beautiful double rainbow appeared against the darkened sky. As I looked at this rainbow I sensed that it was a sign from God to encourage me that he was faithful. I was still on a cocktail of medication, including lithium, so my recovery at home was slow.

Pop had been seeking advice about my condition, and now offered to pay for me to see a Christian psychiatrist in London. Andrew, Maureen and the children accompanied me by train on two or three occasions. Despite glimmers of hope, I was still seeing life in black and white or shades of grey. From the train window I could see fields, trees and houses, but nothing had any real colour. In London, the sessions with the psychiatrist did not bring any breakthrough and there seemed little reason to spend more time and money on further visits. But at the end of the final session, the psychiatrist opened his Bible and read me this verse from the book of Jeremiah: "I know the plans that I have for you" declares the Lord, "plans to prosper you and not to harm you, plans to give you hope and a future." I could see that he was moved nearly to tears as he read this to me, and as I travelled home I wondered if it was still possible for me to start again with God?

The end of the year and Christmas were now approaching. I had not yet been able to face going back to church, and Maureen had also been staying away to protect herself from the pain of more rejection. We decided to attend the "carols by candlelight" service one Sunday evening, just before Christmas. The church was beautifully lit by flickering candles, and the service consisted of a sung carol followed by a reading from the Bible. Each time a reading was given and I heard again the gospel story, I felt my emotions stirring and tears coming to my eyes. I knew this was the loving touch of God and it was the first time for many months that I had felt it. I was greatly encouraged. I had been lied to by the devil all along! God had been true to his word that he would never leave me nor forsake me. I didn't know why I had been allowed to go through that hell on earth, but I now knew that there was hope for the future. After this experience, my healing progressed much faster. Colour came back into my life and soon I was well enough to reduce medication. But I was to stay on lithium.

By this time, Pop was expanding his business, which manufactured greenhouse structures. Pop decided to purchase a piece of land near Winchester which was currently in use as a plant nursery. It was a beautiful location, with a river running alongside the nursery. He planned to design and build a brand-new garden centre, as a working showpiece for his company. During the negotiations, the vendor agreed to allow me come to the nursery for a couple of hours each day to help with pricking-out seedlings and other light jobs around the site. This gave me some feeling of usefulness. After a few months, when the sale of the land was completed, we continued to buy and sell plants and other produce from the existing little shop while the new structure was under construction. During these months, I was well enough to work for longer periods and I began to serve customers, cash up daily takings, and price up items for sale.

By the following Easter, the time had arrived for the "Grand Opening". The new garden centre was a big enterprise. In addition to the large shop building and outdoor plant-sales area, the dwelling- house had been converted into a coffee shop/restaurant, and an upstairs flat. A general manager and plant manager had been recruited, as well as other staff. I was given the title of "Administrator." We were now seeing much higher numbers of customers and were opening seven days per week. I had come around full-circle. Despite all that had happened previously, I was once again working in the family business and I was happy in this working environment.

Chapter 15

"Danger Zone."

David, our son, was now nearly five years old and was due to start school next term. We still lived near the centre of town in the house which had previously been my bachelor-pad. We decided that it would be good for us to move to a house on a new development on the edge of the town. Nearby was a primary school which had a place available for David. It was a big step for me to take, but as my health improved I felt a sense of excitement. We felt it was right to make a fresh start in a new home. The sale and purchase went through quite quickly and we moved into our new home just in time for David to start school.

A few months earlier, during my second period in hospital, Maureen had felt lonely and isolated. She had met an American lady called Norma, whose husband worked for a computer company near Winchester. Norma visited her at home and also took Maureen and the kids shopping and on outings. This seemed to be a wonderful blessing, but over time, Maureen began to form a strong mother-bond with her. Later Norma's husband was recalled to America with his job and she had return with him. Maureen had become so bonded to her that the loss of this friend left a gaping hole in her emotions and a dark feeling of depression and loss began to grip her. During the following eighteen months Norma flew over two or three times and stayed with us in our new house. However relationships between us all were becoming very strained. Norma had hangups and addictions of her own and she was becoming increasingly domineering with Maureen and critical towards the children, both of whom now disliked her. Maureen was torn in her emotions, but each time that Norma left to return to America, Maureen became depressed once again.

I too was finding the situation stressful and rejecting. Maureen would tend to be quiet and depressed when Norma was not around and pre-occupied when she was with us. Both of these situations were upsetting for me. I felt unloved and unappreciated and I experienced strong temptations to look elsewhere for sexual touch and affection. I knew that any relationship with a man or a woman outside of marriage would probably spell the end of our marriage and family together. I felt lonely inside but held on to my faith in God, so I was able to remain faithful to Maureen and pray for breakthrough for us.

A new Curate and his wife had arrived at the church. Bob and Val were very kind and supportive to Maureen during her dark times. They also had a young family and often invited Maureen and the kids to visit and have games and a light meal together. This helped Maureen to feel more accepted by the church.

Norma made a final visit to our home, and this time the situation reached crisis point. Maureen became emotionally torn between wanting her to leave and needing her to stay. David and Esther were becoming increasingly fearful and upset by her words and actions, and eventually I lost my temper with her and told her to leave. That same day, Maureen asked for advice from an experienced couple in Christian counselling, and later that day the lady tried to speak to Norma by phone about her relationship with Maureen and the family. Norma reacted very badly to this conversation and to the advice she was given. She went upstairs, packed her suitcase and left abruptly. She returned to America and was never to return. At first, Maureen was relieved to see her go and tensions in the family eased. But soon the mother-wound inside sent her spiralling back down into depression and despair. I tried to encourage her and help her through this, as did Bob and Val, but one evening when I was at an FGBMFI chapter meeting, Maureen could bear the pain no longer. Her mum was in hospital at the time and Maureen had agreed to keep some pills for her. Not knowing what they were, Maureen swallowed the entire contents of the bottle and went to bed. She didn't tell me about this when I returned home, but by morning she was having strange feelings in her head and limbs. Now feeling fearful, she told me what she had done. I telephoned a doctor and explained what had taken place. He said that she should be alright in a few hours but by late afternoon she was feeling very strange in her body and her heart was racing. I called for an ambulance for her, as I couldn't leave the kids unattended. Once she was in hospital the doctors were shocked that she had not been brought in earlier. They said they would do their best but that she was at high risk of heart failure. She spent the whole night with a nurse in attendance, wired up to a monitor, which showed her heart was beating at an alarmingly high rate. She prayed to God to forgive her for taking the pills and to let her live. Gradually her heartbeat slowed and the danger passed, but after a visit from a hospital psychiatrist, it was decided to admit her to a psychiatric hospital for assessment. Maureen was transferred to Marchwood hospital, the very same place where I had previously been treated. Maureen still had a fear of hospitals, so after a couple of days she managed to persuade the psychiatrist that she would not try to take pills again, and she was allowed home.

After this shock, Maureen started to come to terms with her feelings of loss and abandonment. We had booked to go on a Christian summer camp in August with others from our church. Amongst our group on the camp-site were two young men who had recently been dismissed from teacher-training college for drug-taking. Both had just become Christians but needed accommodation. To our surprise, Maureen and I both felt that we should offer a room in our house to one of them, as we now had a spare bedroom. Another family offered a room to the other young man. We knew we were taking a risk but the young man whose name was Chris, turned out to be a great blessing to us. He was very zealous in his new faith and we would all talk, read the Bible and pray together. He felt blessed by being part of a family and he and his girlfriend were very good with our kids and would sometimes baby-sit for us. It was helpful for Maureen and I to have another person around the house and the kids loved Chris and Jo. Chris was always willing to give us space as a family when we needed it. Our family grew still further during this year. Firstly a friend unexpectedly gave us a one year old tabby cat called "Ziggy". Esther became particularly fond of her. Later that year we received a phone call from one of Maureen's relatives, begging us to take a puppy that they couldn't cope with because she was "messing" everywhere. We agreed, and we went to collect "Lady" from their house. She had been badly treated and was nervous and fearful, so we spent time petting her and praying for her. When David and Esther returned from school, they were excited to find her at home. She quickly bonded with us, and never repeated the messing which she had previously done. Maureen and I both loved dogs, so it was helpful to us to have one in the family. After swiping Lady on the nose with her paw, Ziggy soon became the boss and Lady was no bother to her.

Esther was at school, but David was having difficulties there. He was restless in classes and found it difficult to relate to the other children. We could tell that something was not right, but we didn't know what. Other kids would make fun of David and sadly, this rubbed off on Esther too. It was becoming difficult to get them to school. Then Maureen had an idea, and she applied for a job at the school as a "lunchtime supervisory assistant", commonly called a dinner lady, for one hour per day. To her surprise, she got the job for five lunch periods per week. This enabled her to watch over our kids at lunch-break and also gave her a sense of worth and a small income. We were doing better now as a family. However, the costs of our home and family were rising, so we were forced to borrow more money on the mortgage than we could afford. Eventually, after praying about our financial situation, we felt that we should move to a smaller house nearby. Chris and Jo were planning their wedding and would soon be moving on, so we placed our house for sale. We found a smaller house nearby which we liked, and the owners were looking for something bigger. We were able to arrange an exchange. It was a tight squeeze getting our family and belongings into a three bedroom terraced house but once settled in, we felt happier there. We now had a smaller mortgage and some savings.

I attended one or two healing conferences as suggested to me by Peter, a while ago. One such conference was held in Hertfordshire, and featured a couple called Chris and Lisa. They began with worship, followed by teaching about the love of God the Father, and there were opportunities to receive prayer ministry. Standing out in my memory was a moment when Lisa asked the room-full of people if anyone had ever contemplated suicide. "Be honest if you can," she said, "and raise a hand if that's you." I raised a hand, expecting to be one of just a handful of responders, but to my amazement almost every person in the room raised a hand. I had thought I was weak and selfish, but now I realised just how many people, even in the church, can suffer with hopelessness and despair. Lisa couldn't pray one-to-one with so many people so she prayed a prayer for everyone together, that God would replace death with life.

There was a similar prayer at another, much smaller conference near Oxford, which Maureen attended with me. There was a lady there with a name badge which read "Mary".

She smiled at Maureen during the evening meal and again at breakfast. Maureen felt blessed but wondered who she was and what her motives were. As the conference started, we discovered that she was one of the main speakers. Her talk was about healing of trauma and bad memories, and at the end she had some "words of knowledge" about certain people who were in the room. Maureen felt an urge to go forward for prayer in response, and as Mary prayed she spoke *LIFE* instead of death over Maureen. As she said these words Maureen felt a bolt of electricity go through her, causing a shaking sensation in her body. This was the start of what would be a process of healing for her.

A recession had started in the nation at that time, with very high interest rates on borrowed money. The family business was under threat. My father had retired, and meanwhile, Andrew had taken command of the main company. During the previous year, when business was good, he had invested in a new and bigger factory site and offices. But now, as the recession grew, the value of the site dropped sharply and the interest on the repayments grew alarmingly. The company battled on for several months, but eventually had to be put into receivership. A buyer was found for the new garden centre as a going concern. As the new owners were preparing to take over, they promised to keep all existing staff, including me. But once in charge, they asked me to work seven days a week for six weeks. I tried my best to serve them as a good servant to a new master. When they realised that I was not leaving of my own accord, they called me in to their office: "We understand that you have had mental health problems in the past," the new owner said. "We do not feel that you will be able to achieve the level of workload anticipated during our planned expansion, so we are releasing you from your job with a "golden handshake."

I felt devastated by this action but was forced to leave immediately. Once again I was unemployed. However, we had already booked as a family to attend a prayer rally the following weekend and my spirits were lifted during this event. I felt God tell me not to fear, but to trust that he had my future planned. I succeeded in getting temporary work assignments via an agency and I attended a course to learn how to use a computer. The following year, I was accepted for a year's contract at the High Street branch of a large bank, as a telephone call-handler, while they prepared to open a local call-centre.

During this year, our son David was diagnosed with "Aspergers Syndrome." This helped us to understand David better. He was very intelligent with an amazing memory but sleeping was still one of his problems. David was now thirteen and the time had come for him to move up to the senior school, which had a good special-needs department.

By this time, there were several boys aged twelve to fourteen who came to our house to visit David. I found that my attraction towards boys of this age-group was still strong. I was attracted to two or three of these friends in particular and enjoyed having them visit us. I even felt inside as if I was the same age as them and secretly wished they were my friends. This was a dangerous time for me, as I was tempted to join in with games and horseplay, which could easily have led me into compromising situations. Although I resisted any wrong-doing with them, I felt bad and guilty for having such thoughts. I kept confessing them to God and asking his forgiveness. I knew that these thoughts undermined my relationship with Maureen, which was still lacking romance. I often asked God to heal me and give Maureen and I romantic love and attraction towards each other, and I believed that he was promising me that this would happen, but that it would be in his timing.

During this time Maureen's mother had been unwell for a few months and she was admitted to a psychiatric building, within the main hospital complex. Maureen and I visited her regularly and could see a steady physical and mental deterioration in her. One morning, Maureen woke with an urgent sense that she should go to the hospital. Unfortunately, she was distracted by a telephone call and was delayed in reaching the hospital. On arrival she was told that her mum was in the accident and emergency department but Maureen was not permitted to see her right then. Her mum had suffered a cardiac arrest while being moved across to A&E, and they were trying to resuscitate her. They succeeded in re-starting her heart but she did not regain consciousness. She spent the next few days on a life-support machine. She showed no vital signs of life so she was declared brain-dead. After gaining the agreement of all close family members, the machine was switched off, and after a few hours she finally slipped away.

Thankfully we had witnessed her mum accept Christ a few years before. Although Maureen had never enjoyed a proper mother-daughter relationship, she was plagued by feelings of guilt that she had not been with her mum when she had the cardiac arrest. There was also a feeling of loss and grief over all the things which might have been different, if her mum had not been so mentally unwell during most of her life. During this time of grieving, Maureen met a lady called Alice who lived near us. Alice liked dogs and took an interest in Lady. By this time Lady's health was deteriorating, and we were recommended to contact a professor of veterinary medicine at Bristol University. We took Lady to see him, and he asked if he could take her on as an experimental case at minimum cost, as he was very keen to discover the reasons for her condition. This involved several trips to the Bristol area. It was a long journey for Maureen to make on her own, so Alice offered to take Maureen and Lady there in her car, while I was at my work. Alice became close friends with Maureen and used to visit our home quite often. I could see that Maureen was becoming very reliant on her.

Chapter 16

"Self-Employed!"

The year was 1999; the next millennium was fast approaching. My contract with the bank had been extended by a few months. As it drew to an end I was again looking for another job. I went to visit Pop, who had now moved into a private residential home. He told me that he had found a potential job opportunity for me. He said he had placed an advertisement in a local newspaper without telling me, in which he was offering a financial incentive to anyone who might want to employ me. My initial thoughts were that he was just interfering in my life and that God would lead me to find the right job. However Pop had received a response from a lady who ran an Estate Agency business with two local branches. I was curious and agreed to meet her. She seemed to like me and agreed with Pop to take me on for a trial period. A few days later I started work in her office. The work she required was basic and monotonous but I was picking up information and observing her dealings with clients. After the trial period was over she agreed to employ me on a monthly wage, partly subsidised by Pop.

After a few more weeks, she wanted to transfer me to her other branch in Chandlers Ford, which was a sprawling area of housing, halfway between Winchester and Southampton. This branch was managed by her son Shaun, a man in his thirties who had originally trained as a master-butcher. I started to work there and we both got on well. It wasn't long before he was sending me out of the office to accompany viewings and even make straight-forward property valuations. When Shaun and his family took a fortnight's summer holiday, I was able to find buyers for two of his properties and take on two others "For Sale". On his return from holiday, Shaun was very pleased with my efforts and we continued to work together as a team.

Later that year I had a chance meeting with a local property surveyor who had an office in Fair Oak, a village about five miles away. He had also dabbled in estate agency but wanted to give up that part of his business due to lack of available time. I asked if I could take over the estate agency part of the business and he agreed to discuss details. I talked it over with Shaun but he and his mother were not keen to take on a third branch. However they were willing to let me take it on myself, especially if we shared some properties and the commission from them. I went to see Pop and talked matters over with him. I explained that I would be renting the shop and the furniture, so the starting outlay of cash would only be required for items like signage and stationery. Pop agreed to advance me some money to get started. We agreed that if I failed to make a success of this venture there would be no great financial loss.

By January 2000, I had opened the new office, having repainted the walls and re-carpeted the floor. I had designed a logo and had received new "For Sale" boards and stationery, as well as new signage for the front of the shop. To start with I had no new properties of my own to sell but the surveyor had passed over to me a handful of properties, which were still on his books, on a commission sharing basis. My new shop window opened with those properties plus some properties in Chandlers Ford to be shared with Shaun. To my great relief, I soon began to do valuations and take on properties from the village and nearby area. My honest approach seemed to make up for my lack of experience. I employed a Saturday assistant and a weekday assistant in the office, as I was often out of the office doing valuations or viewings. I learned to do the photographing of houses, the measuring-up and the preparation of sales brochures. The work was often stressful but also exciting. Having been told that I would never work again, here I was running my own business.

At first, I was driving seven miles to and from Winchester every day in an elderly car. Maureen was feeling that a move to a cheaper area would help us financially, and David was due to finish school that summer. Esther was now at senior school with David but was unhappy due to being bullied. Both of them had been taking time off school which was causing us stress and pressure. We found a place for Esther in a Christian school located in the same village as my office. We decided the time was right to move house again. We sold our terraced house in Winchester and were able to buy a semi-detached house about half a mile from my office. After David had completed his GCSE exams, we moved house. It took Maureen and David a few months to settle into this new area but the new location was ideal for me. Esther was also much happier in her new school.

Maureen had recently passed her driving test so I was able to buy her a small car in good condition. As my business progressed I sold my old car and took out a lease on a new car for the business. We also joined the local village church and a local home-group for mid-week fellowship. We were better accepted by the people in this church and Maureen and I started to grow again in our faith. David had taught himself guitar and bass, and now displayed a gifting for playing and singing with the worship band. This was a more secure time for our family.

Sadly, Lady's condition was worsening year by year and further visits to the college near Bristol became necessary. Maureen was afraid to drive that distance by herself, so Alice took them both in her car. Alice was becoming increasingly involved with us as a family. She had never been married or had children, and was rather lonely. She would try to help with all kinds of things. I was grateful for her help and accepted the fact that she and Maureen spent time together. By the year 2002, Lady's condition was poor, and the time came when she was suffering too much. We drove to Bristol with Alice, in two cars. We all knew that the day had come to say goodbye to Lady. We accompanied the vet into a consulting room and he prepared to give her an injection. I held her paw and prayed silently as the injection was given. Maureen was so deeply upset that she stood in a corner, shaking and unable to look. On the journey home Maureen was very silent and Esther was tearful. We had all loved Lady but Maureen had become especially bonded. There had been many times when she had held Lady in her arms to relieve her own childhood pain. Maureen sank into a depressed mood once more, having no dog to care for. I tried to comfort her and Alice spent time with her regularly, for which I was grateful. After a few weeks we decided that the best therapy would be to get another dog. One morning I woke up having had a vivid dream about a dog. In the dream I had seen a brown and white dog rolling onto its back to have its' tummy tickled. I told Maureen about the dream and we decided to drive to a nearby town where we knew they had a sanctuary for abandoned and unwanted dogs. However after looking at all the dogs, there was not one that fitted the description in the dream. We had felt positive that this would be the day to find our new dog so we arrived back home at lunch-time feeling very disappointed. Then Maureen remembered seeing an advertisement in the local paper which she had since thrown in the bin. We were able to retrieve the newspaper and she looked through the classified adverts.

"This is the one!" she exclaimed. "Liver and white Springer-Spaniel puppies for sale, and there's a phone number too." I phoned the number and a man answered. "I've only got one puppy left," said the man, "and he's a boy." He went on to say that he only sells puppies to people who can really look after them properly. I explained about our previous dog Lady; how we had nursed her through poor health and how desperate my wife was for another dog. "Tell you what," replied the man, "I like the sound of you and your family. Would you like to come and see the puppy?" "Could we come this afternoon?" I replied. The answer was yes, so off we went again to a town in the opposite direction. The puppy was very cute and just eight weeks old. He was liver and white, and of stocky build. The man had the puppy's mother and grandmother there at his home. Then the grandmother dog, also liver and white, came over to me with her tail wagging. I stroked her head and suddenly, she rolled onto her back to have her tummy tickled. I remembered my dream and thought I heard a voice say; "Like grandmother, like grandson."

We arranged to collect him in two weeks time, after a visit to summer camp. So two weeks later we went to collect him. He became part of our family and we named him "Sam."

Chapter 17

"Heart Attack."

By November 2002, Sam was nearly six months old. He was a well built "working-springer" and could already pull strongly when walking on his lead. One Sunday morning, Maureen and I had decided to take him for a walk in a country park. This park had a miniature steam railway which operated at weekends, giving rides to both adults and children. It had been raining a lot over previous days and the ground was wet and slippery. I was feeling tired and irritable, as if I was going down with the flu. Maureen had put Sam on his lead in case he ran across the railway track, when suddenly he pulled hard on her arm. She slipped on the muddy surface and slid down a bank with him. She cried out in pain as her leg was twisted under her. I tried without success to pull her back up. Then I decided to go for help, but I had to climb over a low fence first. As I did so, I felt something like a heavy weight hit me in the chest. Gasping for air, I reached the park road leading down towards a lake. In front of me I could see the building with the miniature railway station and a cafe inside it. It was about two hundred yards away. I struggled to reach this building, still gasping for breath. As I arrived, there was a woman just inside the station who had seen me coming. She guessed immediately that I was having a heart attack because her husband, the engine-driver, had once experienced a similar event. She hurried over and helped me lie down on a bench, while her husband also came over. I managed to tell them that Maureen had slipped down a bank with our dog. They had a telephone there in the building and somebody phoned 999 for an ambulance. The husband stayed with me while the woman and her teenage son went to look for Maureen and Sam. Miraculously there was an empty ambulance passing close by, and within a minute or two I had two ambulance paramedics attending me. They quickly evaluated the situation and lifted me by a special chair onto a bed inside the vehicle. As they drove me away from the building, I could see the woman helping Maureen along the road and her son holding Sam on his lead. At least I knew they were safe.

One of the paramedics gave me aspirin to chew, but the heavy weight remained and I was still breathing with short gasps. I could tell that the two men were very concerned as I had not responded to their efforts to stabilise me. I then prayed silently to God, and said; "Lord, if this is my time, I am ready to come to you. But I don't want to die. There is still so much that I haven't done, and Maureen and the family need me."

After a fifteen minute journey I arrived at Southampton General Hospital. I was carried in and placed on a bed; I saw the faces of about ten people, all gathered round the bed. Then I must have blacked out. When I woke up I was in a "high-dependency" ward. I learned later that I had experienced a full-blown heart attack right there in the emergency department, and that they had used clot-busting drugs to save my life.

Meanwhile, back at the park, Maureen had been attended to by a "first-responder" paramedic, who had arrived on the scene just as my ambulance was leaving. She had injured her leg but nothing was broken. She had refused their offer to take her to the hospital for an X-ray, because she did not want to leave Sam. The poor dog was very frightened and anxious, knowing instinctively that something was seriously wrong. He stood shaking and whimpering next to her. Maureen phoned Alice who came in her car to take them both home. Now they had to break the news about me to David and Esther. They too were shocked and alarmed by the news.

Maureen phoned my brother Andrew, who at first, thought she was exaggerating about my condition. However about half an hour later, he arrived at our house and drove Maureen and the kids to the hospital, while Alice stayed behind with Sam. On arrival at A&E they were told that I had been moved to a special ward following a heart attack. As they reached this ward, I had just woken up. I felt weak and sleepy but I was alive! The family spent a few minutes with me but I was drifting in and out of consciousness.

Over the course of the next few days my family visited regularly and brought me a portable CD player and head-phones, together with three of my favourite worship and soaking CD's. I was being kept under observation and was gradually gaining strength; soon I was moved to a ward for patients with heart problems. Unlike my time in Marchwood hospital, I was not in fear and dread. In fact the opposite was true! I felt a great peace over me, and as I began to listen to my music on CD, I received great blessing and anointing from the Holy Spirit. I felt as if I was being lifted before God's throne in heaven, and I received encouraging words about his love for me, and his plans for the future for me and my family. I knew that these promises would happen over time, and not instantly, but hope and faith were re-kindled in my heart.

After a few more days in hospital, I had a "stent" inserted into one of my arteries near the heart. I was told that this artery was almost completely blocked, and the stent would open it up to allow more blood to flow through. Shortly afterwards I was allowed to leave the hospital, but my recovery would be gradual over a few weeks. As there would be too much activity and pressure on me at home, it was agreed for me to spend three weeks with Andrew and his wife, convalescing. This arrangement worked well. At first I could only walk around their house, then I could stroll a little in their garden, but after a fortnight, I could walk a good distance down the road and back. During this period I was often left on my own and had opportunity to read and listen to music. I was still receiving blessings and peace from God. Finally, after about three weeks, I was strong enough to return to my family, who were delighted to have me back home again.

During my time away from home, Maureen had felt lonely and anxious. Alice had offered to move in with the family, and she stayed the entire six weeks. During this time, she helped Maureen with many household duties, accompanying her on dog walks, shopping and outings with the children. This was a great help, but once again Maureen was becoming bonded and reliant on another woman to help fill the need for a mother figure. On my return, Alice moved back to her own home, but Maureen continued to meet with her often, and she was frequently with us in our home. It was therefore difficult for me to spend much personal time with my wife, and we still lived rather like close friends, sharing family and accommodation. We still had very little romantic or sexual interaction. Maureen had been so abused by men during her childhood years that she found a man's loving touch threatening. I was very fond of her, but my sexual inclinations were still inclined towards men. Yet we both knew that God had made his love towards us very clear, even in our brokenness.

At this time, an unusual event took place. Sam was about a year old by now, and could normally be let off his lead safely in walking areas. I had started walking him again myself. One morning, I took him to the nearby woods, a favourite place of his, but on this occasion he was startled by a sound like a gun-shot coming from inside the woods. Frightened by this loud noise, he ran at full speed straight past me, heading back towards our house. I shouted for him to stop, but the louder I shouted, the more frightened he became. He just kept on running. My heart was in my mouth. There was a busy main road between the woods and our house; if Sam ran into this road he would probably be run over and killed by speeding traffic. I knew that Maureen would be devastated if Sam was killed, but all I could think to do was to send up an arrow prayer to God; "Please rescue Sam!" I prayed; "Please don't let him die."

I ran towards the busy main road, dreading what I might find. To my amazement, there on the grass verge was a man of at least sixty years of age, wearing a jacket and shorts with a rucksack on his back. His right arm was lowered towards the ground, and in his right hand he was holding a dog by its collar. The dog looked peaceful and calm; it was Sam!

"I think this is your dog," said the man quietly, "He was in the road." Shocked, relieved and embarrassed, I came over and leant down to put Sam back on his lead. Then I stood up to thank the man, wondering how he had managed to catch a frightened dog by its collar on a busy road. I looked up, but the man was gone. I looked all around, but he had vanished; there was no sign of him anywhere in view. I had heard that others had seen angels dressed like ordinary people, and when I reached home, I told Maureen what had happened. I told her that the man with the rucksack must have been an angel, sent in answer to my desperate prayer. She agreed.

After about four months of absence, I was able to return to my work. My assistant had managed to keep the office open with the help of one of my clients, a retired policeman, who voluntarily gave his time to help in the office. I felt very blessed by his action. There had been no additional properties added, though some had sold. I had been advised by family and friends that the stresses of running the business were not good for my heart, so I made the decision to try to sell. After a few weeks of unsuccessful efforts, my assistant asked if she could take it over with her brother who was due to be returning from abroad. I agreed, but it would be many months before she and her brother concluded the arrangements.

Chapter 18

"Torment and Toronto."

I was now spending my final months running my business. Times had become much harder in the country and property prices were now falling. Spring had turned into summer, and while I was working, Maureen was still seeing Alice frequently. She knew she had become over-dependent, but could not find a way to change things. We had booked another visit to the summer camp in early August, but this time we were not camping. We had been forced to book our group into two guest-houses, located very close to one-another. We drove down in two cars, having left Sam in the care a close friend, who was staying in our house. On arrival, Maureen, Esther and Alice checked in to one guest-house, and David and I shared a room at the other one.

During the first night, Maureen and Alice had a big upset. Alice announced that she wanted to end their friendship, and that she was leaving in the morning. Early the next morning, Esther came over to where David and I were staying; she looked very worried. Esther told us to come over as soon as possible. When we arrived, we found Maureen in an agitated state and Alice was very silent. Soon after that, Alice left in her car. Meanwhile I tried to calm the situation. I had to explain to both hosts that we had an emergency, and were forced to leave immediately and return home. I was very stressed and anxious about Maureen, and also angry and disappointed to miss the summer camp, and the blessings I was hoping we might have received.

The next few weeks were very difficult. Though Maureen understood as an adult that she and Alice had to be separated, yet the childhood emotions of rejection and abandonment were overpowering. She became very mentally ill, despite the efforts of family, friends and her doctor to help her. Over the following weeks, she went missing from home on several occasions, usually taking Sam with her in her car. She was often to be found near Alice's house, having swallowed alcohol and pills after Alice had refused to speak to her. On one such occasion, I received a phone call at the office that she was missing again. After collecting the children from home, we drove about and found her car, which was parked at a spot near a river. In fear and anxiety, we walked up the nearby river bank wondering if we would find her body floating in the water. It was a frightening time for us all. Slowly Maureen began to adjust to her situation, but her mental state was still very fragile.

We found a programme on "God TV" from a church in Toronto, Canada. Over there, they were experiencing wonderful blessings and miracles from God, and we had both been encouraged by watching these programmes. We decided to try to send Maureen to this church, and I made contact with their church-office by phone. They were very helpful and compassionate about our situation. They encouraged Maureen to come, and arranged for a lady to meet her off the plane to take her to her hotel and accompany her at the church. We booked the plane tickets for Maureen to go for a week, and for Esther to join her three days later, after finishing her exams. The day before she was due to travel, Maureen made one final attempt to visit Alice to ask for forgiveness, and seek reconciliation before her trip to Canada. The visit was unwise and unhelpful. I received a phone call from Maureen on her mobile phone. She sounded drugged and disorientated, but she managed to tell me that she was parked at the side of a main road some distance away, and that she had swallowed all her pills. In a panic, I phoned the police, who agreed to look for her, and I set out with David in my car. Thankfully, Sam was with me on that occasion. It took me over half an hour to reach the place, and I spotted her car in a lay-by, but it was empty. I phoned the police and, to my relief, was told that they had found her and she was in a nearby hospital. I imagined that the hospital would pump out her stomach to flush out the pills, and then admit her into a psychiatric ward. I thought that our plans for Toronto would have to be abandoned. However, to my surprise, the hospital decided to send her home with me. Maureen was still very fragile, and it seemed impossible for her to travel the next day. We didn't even try to pack her suitcase, and I put her to bed to try to get some sleep. I also had some fitful sleep, only to be woken by Maureen at about four o'clock in the morning.

"God has told me that I must go;" she said. "It's a matter of life or death!" I didn't know what to do for the best, but decided that if God said it, we must do it. We stumbled around, packing her things for the trip, and I left a note for David and Esther to tell them what was happening. So, off we went to Heathrow airport!

Somehow, Maureen made the trip to Canada, though she was almost detained in the immigration department at Toronto airport. Fortunately, a very kind lady from the church was waiting for her, took her to her hotel and settled her in. The next morning, Maureen felt a peace over her and was able to walk a short distance to the church, where she was warmly welcomed. During that day she was looked after by several ladies, and that evening, an older lady spent two hours praying with her, holding her by the hand, and comforting her. Maureen could sense the presence of God and the love of these people, and she began to feel more hopeful. The following day, she was accompanied to an area of the building where they had healing and prophecy rooms. Again she was ministered to and received further encouragement. That evening, to her surprise, people started to arrive at the church carrying cushions and pillows. "Excuse me," Maureen said, to one of her new friends; "Are all these people staying here for the night?" "Oh no," she replied, "tonight is a "soaking" evening at the church."

Maureen didn't understand what that meant. Soon afterwards, a worship team began to play gentle music, and Maureen was given a pillow, and tried to lie on the floor as the others were doing. It had been explained to her that she should try to focus on Jesus, and allow his Holy Spirit to minister and speak to her. She was rather restless and found this difficult to do, until the leader of the worship group came over and knelt next to her, speaking encouraging and peaceful words from God over her. He was followed by a lady with a violin, playing beautiful music over her, and speaking more words of encouragement and of God's love. Although still fragile, Maureen felt a sense of heat going deep inside her being, and peace and hope returning.

The following day, Esther was due to arrive. I had taken her to the airport, and now stayed at home to look after David and Sam. Meanwhile, Esther arrived in Toronto, and Maureen was able to meet her at the airport. They were able to attend some of the meetings together and also to do some sight-seeing. Esther was going through a difficult time herself, and she found some of the worship difficult to cope with. But it was helpful for Maureen to have Esther's company there. After a week in Canada, they both made the return journey to Heathrow. I was there with David and Sam to collect them. I could tell that Maureen had greatly benefited from her time in Toronto, but once home again, things started to slip backwards. There was no similar fellowship that we knew of locally. After prayer and discussion, we decided to make a return trip to

Canada with the whole family. We were able to find a host family for Sam, and in late October we all flew back to Toronto. We were there together for two weeks, and during this time received much blessing and encouragement. We all had healing prayer and prophetic words from God. In addition we enjoyed the fiery preaching of a young Canadian man, who had come from a very disadvantaged background. He was now seeing healings and miracles following his preaching. The worship was anointed and powerful, and we also took part in further soaking sessions. At the end of the fortnight, I had been very blessed, and we returned home refreshed and with more faith.

We were so pleased with our visit that we made plans for Maureen to return for a third visit after New Year, and perhaps stay there for three months or so, receiving healing and ministry, while the rest of us took turns to visit for a week or two. This would have been expensive, although someone had offered us the use of an empty apartment. Maureen and Esther flew out in January, but found the weather extremely cold, and there were no special events happening at the church. After two or three days, they were feeling homesick and decided to come home. I think this time we had tried to run ahead of God and had followed our own plan. Fortunately, at this disappointing time, we discovered a church in the Midlands which was holding meetings of a similar nature. We arranged to attend a conference in Dudley, near Birmingham. The visiting speaker was the same young Canadian whom we had seen in Toronto. The conference was exciting and trip was well worthwhile. As a family we received encouragement and impartations of healing and faith, as well as enjoying a powerful sense of worship. On our return, Maureen was feeling stronger again, and I was also strengthened and encouraged.

Meanwhile, Pop's health was now failing. He had reached the age of 88, and had been restricted to a wheelchair for some time due to a gradual loss of balance. He was being cared for in a beautiful residential home. By mid-April, his organs were failing and all the family members were preparing for his death. He had resisted our attempts to share the gospel with him over many years, but in the last few days of his life he allowed Esther to share a few words at his bedside. Although he was drifting in and out of consciousness by this time, he heard her pray a simple "sinner's prayer" on his behalf, inviting Jesus into his life. She asked him to squeeze her hand if he had also prayed this prayer, and she felt his hand squeeze hers. I was delighted when she told me this, as I had been praying for him to accept Jesus before he died. On April 21st, Pop passed away peacefully in his sleep. Later that same day, I read Psalm 91 in my Bible, and I received a strong sense from God that Pop was now with Jesus, and that God was pleased with us.

Pop had requested a cremation service, followed by a reception at a local hotel. The whole family were present at the service, as well as other close friends. Although funerals are often sad and sombre occasions, I had an unexpected experience. During the singing of a hymn, I was aware of the presence of the Holy Spirit. I felt as if I was looking up into heaven, and that Pop was already there with Jesus. Under my breath, I spoke to him, and said; "Pop, I'm so glad you made it to heaven. I have forgiven you and I look forward to seeing you again one day." As I did this, I felt joy in my spirit, and a release of my fear of him which had haunted me for years. Instead, I felt a love for him which I had never known before. I had to compose myself in front of the other family members as I wanted to jump up and shout "Hallelujah!" My father had been a dominant figure in my life, and now he had passed away. I would miss him, but I was also released from his controlling influence.

My final year at the business was a struggle, with house-sales slowing down and properties to sell hard to find. My earnings from the business were poor, and we had to use up our remaining savings. I was anxious that my assistant might change her mind about taking over the business, but she still seemed confident that things would improve.

At the end of this year, in November, we had planned one more trip to Canada. Sadly, David was unwell before we were due to depart, and Maureen had to stay behind with him. However I still went with Esther and with three other ladies. This was an important trip for me, as I received much encouragement. At the end of one meeting, people were asked to come to the front of the building to receive ministry. However, I went on my own right to the very front where there was an altar and a large wooden cross. The Holy Spirit met with me there, and I stood weeping and sobbing for about forty-five minutes. During this time, I was talking to God and receiving from him in my spirit. Even though I was sobbing and grief was being healed, at the same time I was feeling wonderful love and joy.

We had been feeling that a move back to Winchester would be good for us, as I would no longer have a business to run. We began the process of selling our house and looking for one in Winchester. We found a property to purchase once the probate was through, but our present house took longer to sell than we expected. I finished at the office just before Christmas, as my former assistant and her brother had now taken over the business. At long last, we found a buyer for our current house, so we spent Christmas there, and prepared to move to our new home after the New Year. I now had no job, but I applied to join a course to learn bus-driving.

Chapter 19

"New Horizons."

In mid-January, we moved back to our home town of Winchester. I expected this to be our final move, and a permanent place for us to settle. I hoped that we would find a church where we would be accepted, and where we could grow into the sort of family that God had planned for us to be. With the benefit of my share of inheritance money from Pop's estate, we had moved back to the area where we started from. The house itself had already been extended from three to four bedrooms, and had a larger than average back garden. I invested in a rear paved patio area and a few young fruit trees for the back garden. I expected to live here a long time.

My plans for joining a bus-driving course received a setback. I was due to start in February, but I fell ill with the "flu", and was bed-ridden with a high temperature for nearly two weeks. It took another month before I was fully well. I joined the course in late March, but even though I succeeded in driving a 53-seater coach, I soon realised that the stress of bus driving would be too great for me. I finished the course, but decided instead to apply for a job driving disabled children to and from school in a minibus. It took time to obtain the necessary licence, but by June I had started this job.

Meanwhile, we joined a new church in Winchester, and they were welcoming to us. We were also putting soaking into practice in our house using music CD's which I had purchased in Toronto and in Dudley. We had one or two friends who enjoyed coming for a soaking evening. We didn't experience the anointing that was present in a larger group in Canada, but we did feel the peaceful presence of the Holy Spirit. Maureen and I also discovered an important new key to help with our healing. We started having personal soaking times together, as a couple. We would lie down on our bed and listen to the words and music, trying to focus on the Lord. To start with, we could only hold hands, as tender physical touch was still awkward between us. I realised that Maureen was like a small child in her emotions, so I began to stroke her face and back in the way that a loving parent would do to a baby or little child. During such times, she sometimes let out baby noises or spoke in a child-like tone of voice. I knew that God was using these times to reach some very deep and damaged childhood emotions, including those which had been so stirred up by the rejection of both Norma and Alice. At first, Maureen was unable to touch me in a similar way, but over time she became more able to caress my face and hair. I too found myself feeling like a small child, longing for loving touch and affection.

In June, we attended a small conference in Scotland. This conference was unusual because there were several well-known prophetic speakers from other countries, yet the venue was a tiny prefabricated church building in the middle of a poor housing estate. It was hard to fit everybody into the building, and delegates had to stand in the doorways and even listen from outside. God moved powerfully in this humble setting, and we received further blessing and encouragement.

During the last few months, we had connected our home-computer to the internet for the first time. There were many advantages to this, but also temptations. I discovered that I could easily view video clips of men and boys participating in wrestling. Despite all that God had done for me, I still felt a thrill of sexual excitement from this. Although I was not attracted by hard-core pornography, yet this wrestling had a similar effect on me, and I realised that I still had a sexual addiction. I felt very guilty and ashamed after giving in to it. I knew it was unhelpful to my marriage, yet I felt hooked and craved for more, especially when feeling anxious or lonely. Every time that I tried to break the addiction, I ended up falling into it again. Any momentary thrill would always be followed by guilt and shame. I prayed that God would somehow change my thinking. I received his forgiveness and love, and his assurance that his healing would come to me and to Maureen.

In September, I took David, Esther and a female cousin of theirs to a youth conference in Dudley, called "Joel's Army." They enjoyed the lively worship, singing and dancing and I too was blessed. During one of the meetings I plucked up courage to approach the two young men who were guest speakers from the USA, and briefly told them of my addiction for watching, and becoming sexually excited about young men wrestling. One of these men looked straight at me and said: "Root from childhood, LEAVE in Jesus Name!" I felt something loosen inside, and after turning round to walk back towards the edge of the room, I suddenly started to sob, with tears running down my cheeks. The Lord had done some sort of healing or deliverance. Although I admit that I did not experience total freedom from my addictive habit, I did notice that after this, the level of excitement or compulsion was much reduced.

A month later, a local church in Winchester hosted a "Father Heart of God" conference over a weekend. We were not able to attend every session, but once again the Lord was faithful and compassionate to Maureen and I, and we both received a beautiful touch from his Spirit. I believe that our willingness to confess our sins, ask his forgiveness, and seek his help in forgiving others, was a sign of a humble and contrite heart, which God looks for in his people. We were growing deeper in our relationship with him, even though we still felt inadequate ourselves. The church we had joined had not proved ideal for all the family, so after seeking God, we decided to try out the Vineyard church who had just hosted the weekend conference. After a few more visits, we decided to join this new fellowship.

As this year was drawing to a close, our son David became mentally unwell. We were told that he had a condition where lack of light during winter months triggers a form of depression. This condition, together with his Asperger problem, caused him to become very fearful and anxious. He was prescribed medication by the doctor, and I spent time with him, both in the daytime and at night. I would sometimes lie down next to him and pray with him, putting my arms round him to comfort him. On more than one occasion we sensed the presence of the Holy Spirit.

On the first day of January 2005, in the early hours of the morning, I had been sitting next to David, like I had done when he was a small child. Suddenly he was touched by the Holy Spirit and began speaking prophetically over himself. I too could sense the anointing. I thought this must be the breakthrough moment for him, and rejoiced in my heart. Yet, during the next few days, he became very fearful and despairing once again. Gradually, over the coming few weeks, his condition improved, and by April, he was well enough to begin a school driving job similar to the job that I was doing, until the end of the summer school term.

In June, David and I attended a weekend conference together in Chiswick, London. The theme included healing of emotions. During one of the sessions, the speaker asked the assembled delegates to stand, in order to receive prayer for healing of early year's trauma. He said that there could be someone present who had felt rejection and fear of being born, while still inside their mother's womb. He had hardly spoken these words when, to my shock and surprise, a long loud shriek came out of my mouth. I had not felt any emotion before this happened, but now all eyes were on me. The speaker ran across to where I was standing and put his arms around me from behind. As he did so, I began to weep as God performed an unexpected healing to my infant-emotions. At the end of the session, the speaker asked for volunteers to come to the front to offer hugs to other needy delegates. I went forward immediately and joined about five others at the front. Many people came forward to receive a hug, and I was blessed to be able to give a hug to some of them. I believe that the healing I had just received enabled me to do this for others.

By late July, both David and I joined the team of drivers working for a taxi company at Southampton airport. But in September, I returned to a longer school run while David stayed on at the airport. We had spent money on conferences, as well as living expenses, and now we were running short of money once again. Our inheritance money had been spent on the house, so we were forced to take out a small mortgage. Although I returned to airport driving in January, David had another setback similar to the previous year, and was unable to work for a few weeks.

As my 60th birthday approached, Maureen and I realised that we were falling further into debt, and our only solution seemed to be to sell our house and move back to a cheaper house with lower costs. We prayed and asked God if this was our fault, but he simply replied; "I love you and I have plans for you if you will follow me." So, we started another property search. The house which I thought would be our final home turned out to be the shortest stay of all!

Chapter 20

"Times of Testing."

It was in June 2007. We had sold our house in Winchester to the first viewer at a good price, and God led us to a house in the very same area in which we had lived in during the Estate Agency days. This house was not very attractive to look at and the garden was small, but the Lord told us the house had all the space we needed. And he was right! After paying off our previous mortgage, we still had some money left, which we put on deposit.

We had enjoyed some years of relative plenty and had taken the opportunity to attend conferences and travel to Canada where we had witnessed the miracle-working power of God. We had experienced something of his love and compassion. Times of testing were now coming where our faith and trust in him would grow stronger under trials.

I returned to airport taxi work, while Maureen had recently trained as a "school escort". By September, she had started a school-run, accompanying "special needs" children to and from school and David was employed as her driver. But David had another relapse at Christmas-time, and was unable to continue his job. I decided to give up my work at the airport for a few weeks, in order to take his place on Maureen's school-run. For the next three months, Maureen and David still received wages but I had no income. This first Christmas and New Year period was difficult for us, but David was not as ill as he had been previously. We re-joined the local church in the village of Fair

Oak; we already knew a lot of the people there. As David's health improved again, he was able to play bass guitar and sing in the worship band at some of the services.

On 26th March 2008, Maureen and I celebrated our 25th Wedding Anniversary. We had a meal out together on the day itself, and also a gathering with Christian friends on the following Sunday lunchtime. This took place in a local pub and included a sit-down meal. This was a blessing for us and we received cards and some presents. On the same Sunday the vicar had agreed to include the "Renewing of our Marriage Vows" within the evening service. This was an opportunity to thank God for each-other and to commit again to the rest of our marriage. Over the years together, Maureen and I had often felt the Lord speaking to us through his Spirit. Some of these words had proved accurate, though others had not always worked out the way we expected. The night before our lunchtime celebration, we had a soaking-time together. I felt God's Spirit speak into my heart in a very personal way. The main emphasis of his word to us was as follows: "My son, I know and understand that you and Maureen married without the normal romance and physical attraction, and that you have lived like this during 25 years of marriage. I honour you for this, but now I am about to bring changes that will make it possible for you to love each-other more and be attracted to one-another." He continued by saying that our ministry together would get underway and he would bring his healing to our family. God's timing is different from what we expect and these words are only now, some seven years later, beginning to be realised.

Meanwhile David had started driving with Maureen again, and I returned to airport taxi work. We could no longer afford to attend conferences, and our holidays consisted of short breaks to the Isle of Wight. Even so, after two years had passed fairly uneventfully in this house, and despite our efforts to economise, our savings had become depleted. Living expenses still outstripped income and eventually we found ourselves having to borrow money once again at high interest rates to survive and pay our bills. We prayed and God heard us, but there was no further pot of inheritance money to draw on. In the end, the only way we could see to clear debts and produce some spare cash was to sell our house to an investor, who would rent it back to us as tenants. After praying about this several times, we instructed an Estate Agent whom I knew, and trusted in God to find us such a person. Quite soon a suitable buyer appeared, and by Christmas 2009 we had concluded the arrangements. The price received from the sale was reasonable, though below market value, but at least we got to stay in our home and had funds to clear our loans and invest the balance.

Early in 2010, we saw a leaflet advertising an Evangelist/Healer from India who was coming to a hotel in Southampton for two nights. We felt a push to go to this, and discovered that the meetings had been organised by a church about three miles from our home, which had an Indian pastor. We were blessed by the two nights of ministry, and both Maureen and I felt an attraction in our spirits to the Indian pastor and his wife. Their names were Sanjay and Mary, and a few days later we arranged to visit them at their home. They explained that they had been involved in a growing church movement in India, but that God had told them to come to England, to a place called West End. Sanjay was offered a post as pastor to a small group of Christians, who were already meeting in West End, on the edge of Southampton. We attended a few times and were very impressed. We joined the church and also a home-group which met at Sanjay's house. He had a real pastor's heart, and he was very bold in wanting to try new initiatives, such as the event at the Southampton hotel. But some of the older members seemed less keen about his ideas.

We had not realised how strong this under-current was until, one day, a special church meeting was called, and all the congregation were asked to attend. The meeting took place and to our shock and dismay, various members of the previous leadership began accusing Sanjay of acting against their wishes. The attacks were harsh and unpleasant. The leaders said that the post of pastor had been made on a temporary basis only, and that they were terminating his post with the church. Maureen and I were shocked and angry. We decided to give our support to Sanjay, and not return to the church. Sanjay and Mary continued to hold a Sunday meeting in their own home, and a weekday home-group. A few others from the church joined us in this small house-fellowship. Sadly, after a few more months, Sanjay decided to close down the fellowship and take a secular job. We felt very disappointed about all this, and now found ourselves without a church to attend. We began to feel that Southampton might have the right fellowship for us.

Maureen had now developed stomach pains, which were identified as gall stones. A few months later, she had an operation at Southampton General Hospital. On the day of the surgery she felt very nervous, but she was accompanied by a lady called Karen, who helped calm Maureen's fear of hospitals. Karen was a Christian psychotherapist, who had recently started seeing Maureen for deep-release psychotherapy. These weekly therapy sessions have since helped to bring healing to some broken and damaged parts of her emotions from babyhood and through childhood to her teenage years.

In 2012, our landlord, who now owned the house, approached us to say that he was thinking of selling the property. We could not consider buying back the house, so we began to think and pray about renting elsewhere. Thankfully, we had received some unexpected money and we had enough funds to pay the costs of removals and legal fees on a new rented property.

We had identified a small church which appeared to be suitable for us to attend. So we concentrated our home-search around that general area. We found an older-style semi-detached house which the landlord was currently re-furbishing. We viewed the property, still only partially renovated, and met the landlord. He agreed to rent the house to us subject to references and financial checks. I had reached the retirement age of 65 earlier in this year, and now received the state pension. About eight weeks later, the refurbishment was complete, and the moving date was set.

Chapter 21

"Living in the Wilderness."

In the first week of September, we moved house to the western edge of Southampton. The house was located only a few minute's drive from the General Hospital; this location was to prove very useful. The first few days were busy and tiring, as we unpacked boxes of belongings, moved furniture, fitted shelving and hung curtains and pictures. We registered, as a family, with a doctor's surgery in the nearby suburb of Shirley. After working very hard on the house-move, making it our new home, I began to develop pain in the abdomen and bloating of the stomach. I went to see my new doctor. I explained that I had previously suffered with a bowel condition. He concluded that the stress of moving house had caused this problem to flare up again, and that I might be suffering from acute constipation. He prescribed a course of laxative sachets. After a few more days however, my condition was worsening, and by the last day of September I was suffering from sickness and nausea, as well as pain and bloating. I felt so unwell that I took myself to the Accident and Emergency department of the nearby hospital. I was immediately admitted to a ward, where I was put on a drip, and tests were conducted. After three or four days, having successfully passed some motion, I was discharged back home.

During October, I tried to help with dog-walking and other household duties. But I still felt unwell, and at the beginning of November, I returned to the hospital for a camera examination of the bowel. The procedure was very painful for me, and I was informed that they could not complete the examination due to a blockage. I was sent home with yet more laxatives, but, by the end of November I was re-admitted to hospital with nausea and vomiting. I could no longer keep down any food or pass any motions. Once again I was put on a "nil-by-mouth" regime, while more tests were carried out. After a few days in hospital, it was decided that I needed an investigative operation. They did not know exactly what was wrong with me, so could not prepare me for any anticipated outcome. I felt apprehensive and confused. What was God doing? I was too ill and weak by this time to pray much, or hear from him.

The operation took several hours. When I came round from the anaesthetic, I was informed that I now had a "stoma" and would need to wear a disposable bag. Later that day, the surgeon came to the ward and told me that they had removed a large diverticular lump from my bowel, which had been causing a complete blockage. The surgeon went on to explain that after a few months, it should be possible to reverse the stoma surgery and return me to normal bowel function. I spent a few days in recovery before being allowed home. Tests for cancer had been made, but came back negative. I was grateful to be alive, and as I grew stronger, I was able to thank God for saving my life.

I accepted the use of the disposable bags, however my sense of manhood now felt threatened. I wondered how Maureen would feel about a husband who had an unsightly bag attached to his body. She assured me that she didn't mind, but it became a psychological problem for me. I felt somehow unattractive and dirty, and our fragile sex-life was still further threatened. I had to cling to the promises of God and to the hope of successful reversal surgery.

Shortly before Christmas, while soaking and praying, I received a picture in my mind. I saw myself kneeling before a throne. I could see that I was wounded in the stomach area, but yet I was being "knighted". The Lord was laying his sword on my shoulder; then and I felt him say that I had been wounded in the battle against the enemy, but that he would restore me.

As spring approached, our dog Sam became ill. Towards the end of March he had an epileptic fit. We rushed him to the vet, and they kept him in while they tried some medications, but on his return he was still not himself. Soon the fitting started again every few hours. It was frightening and traumatic to watch the poor dog lying on the floor, shaking, fitting, urinating and frothing at the mouth. We knew this must be the end of his life with us. In the morning, we carried him into the car, and drove to the vet for his final injection. The vet put him to sleep with us all present, and then explained that the cause was almost certainly a brain tumour, and there was nothing more we could have done. Maureen became sad and depressed once more, as part of her life had revolved around caring for and walking with Sam.

Thankfully, we had previously booked a week's holiday on the Isle of Wight. We decided to take this break, which helped to distract Maureen from her feelings of grief and depression. We knew that we needed to get another dog, as both of us love dogs. After our return, Maureen noticed an advertisement on the internet for spaniel puppies for sale near Swindon. We made arrangements to travel there to look at the puppies. It was a cold spring day, and the mother and her remaining puppies were kept in an outside shed and run. As Maureen held one of the puppies in her arms, it was wet and shivering with cold. It looked at her pleadingly, as if asking to be taken home right there and then. Somehow we knew in our hearts that this was the one for us, but we had to leave it behind as it was still too young to leave its mother. Having paid a deposit, we arranged to come back about four weeks later. Maureen and I started to feel happier, knowing that we had found the next dog.

Meanwhile, Esther had persuaded David to take her out in the car, and they had returned later with a tiny kitten. Esther said she would keep the kitten in her bedroom as a "house-cat". She gave her the name "Willow". After about two more weeks Maureen went to collect the puppy, and we named her "Tammy". She settled in with us immediately, but when Tammy and Willow first saw each other, there was a great deal of yapping and hissing! The whole family were very anxious about this, so I decided to spend some time alone in a room with both of them, playing with toys and pieces of ribbon. As Tammy pulled on one end of the ribbon, slowly Willow came to investigate. Curiosity overcame fear and soon both were tugging opposite ends of the same piece of ribbon. Instead of being enemies, they soon became friends.

Then one day tragedy struck. Willow ventured into our back garden, and then, un-noticed by us, walked down a side wall and reached the front driveway. She crossed the road outside and was starting to cross back over, when a speeding car came up the road and struck her. Willow was killed instantly. When Maureen tried to pick her up, it was clear that her neck had been broken. This was a terrible shock, especially for Esther and Maureen, as we had all become very fond of this kitten.

In September 2013, I was admitted to hospital to have reversal surgery. I was excited to think that the bag would no longer be needed. But, to my disappointment, after the operation I discovered that I still had a stoma. There had been a problem with a leak, so I had been given a new stoma from the small bowel. The surgeon assured me that this should be temporary, and final reversal could be done in a few months. I was disappointed, and recovered in hospital for a few days. Once back at home, I soaked with the Lord, and he said to me: "You are like a train, parked in a siding for repairs and refurbishment. After a period of rest and restoration and a thorough overhaul, you will rejoin the main-line track and increase in speed more than you can imagine" This was great encouragement for me to look forward to. Little did I know that it would take much longer than I expected!

Meanwhile, my state pension was insufficient to finance our family's needs, and Maureen had been forced to stop work because of her operation. In desperation I considered filing for bankruptcy, as I could see no way out of our problem. But after contacting a Debt Management company, we entered into a "Debt Management Program".

As I was now fit enough to drive, David and I re-applied for private-hire taxi licences and passed the required tests. By mid-July we both returned part-time to airport taxi driving, sharing the use of a car. I was now out of retirement, and these earnings helped us to survive.

That summer, while making a day-visit to summer camp, I went forward for prayer and received a picture from God. I saw a scene of a shipwreck, and I was in the water, clinging to a floating piece of wood. God was saying that my life felt like a mess, but that he would rescue me if I clung to him. During the next two years, we struggled to keep our heads above water financially. God was faithful, and on several occasions he provided some unexpected gift or benefit to keep us afloat. We were also struggling for fellowship, as the church we had been attending had hit some difficulties. We decided to attend a small Vineyard church, but just as we were beginning to feel part of this fellowship, it was announced that the church was closing as the pastor and his wife were leaving.

We felt rather like the children of Israel, wandering around the desert with no clear pathway ahead. The worship of pagan gods had also come into our home through our daughter Esther. She had felt hurt by the church in earlier years and had always felt an attraction towards alternative spirituality. She was now searching in various occult and pagan pathways. Because of this, we had in our home a variety of her books and artefacts, images and idols. It was difficult for her and for us to co-exist in an atmosphere of opposing beliefs. We did our best to show Esther our love and care, and to pray daily for her. God had given us her name before her birth, a Biblical name. I knew that Esther was chosen to be born, and even though she had turned from him to another pathway, Jesus would never turn away from her, but would pursue her with his love.

Chapter 22

"Pain and Promises"

In January 2014, I attended hospital for a dye test to see if reversal surgery could proceed. I had also developed a hernia near the stoma site. I was given a date for surgery in April, but on the day before the surgery, I received a phone call from the hospital cancelling my operation due to lack of bed space. I was very disappointed, but another date was arranged in May. The due date arrived but the operation was cancelled again. Once more, I returned home feeling frustrated and disappointed. Maureen and I prayed together later that day and the Holy Spirit said to us; "Don't give up. I have great things in store for you in the future. At present you are in a place of lack and distress, but I will deliver you and bless you."

I decided to work through the busy summer period, as the income from taxi-driving was much needed. A new date for reversal surgery and hernia repair was fixed for November. But when the due date arrived, the operation was cancelled yet again. Soon after this I noticed a painful lump in my groin. The doctor confirmed that a second hernia had appeared. In January, a new date was arranged and then cancelled again on the day. Even the surgeon was becoming frustrated and embarrassed by all these cancellations. He offered me a date in early February, but with a different surgeon, as he himself was not available then. This time I made it through to the anaesthetic room which was located next to the operating theatre. The new surgeon came out to speak to me and examine me. He noticed a small lump in my stomach and, as he pressed down on it, I felt some discomfort. He seemed concerned, but continued with the anaesthetic. Later, as I was coming round from the operation, I was conscious of someone leaning over my hospital bed and speaking to me. I wasn't sure if I was awake or dreaming, but I heard a voice say; "I decided to abort the operation in order to have further investigation of the lump."

The man left, and as I regained consciousness, I felt around my stomach. Sure enough, the stoma and the bag were both still there! Later, this surgeon visited me and explained that if the lump was malignant, the operation could have become a disaster area. Once again I went home without any change; once again we prayed, and Holy Spirit said to me; "My son, this will turn out for my glory and my praise. Be strong and of good courage; be not afraid, neither be dismayed. All things will work together for good. I will heal you in my way and in my timing. Keep praising me, and do not give the devil a foothold. Do not accept a negative diagnosis, but lay everything at the foot of my cross, where I shed my blood for your healing."

It was hard to imagine how all this was working for God's glory and my good, but I was encouraged to continue to have faith. I was learning that when something doesn't work out the way I expected, I must simply trust that God is good and he knows all things from beginning to end. Meanwhile, the lump had disappeared and nothing more was said about it.

Later in February, I was called in for a further camera examination. This procedure was very painful for me, and the results were again inconclusive. My healing was still on hold. Was God building my perseverance and faith through trials? I attended the surgeon's clinic in April, when He apologised for the inconclusive results and referred me for a CT scan. I was given the scan, and two weeks later I received a phone call to say that it had been satisfactory and the surgery could go ahead. I was delighted.

Then, to my dismay, I received a phone call telling me that the surgeon had changed his mind. He now wanted me to attend for a stretching procedure under anaesthetic. By this time, I was losing hope of ever having the reversal surgery. Somehow I had to trust that God would heal me completely as he had promised.

I attended hospital for the stretching procedure. But first, I had to have yet another enema. A nurse arrived to administer it, but the pain was so sharp that I cried out and flinched, causing the nozzle to slip and spill most of the enema liquid on the bed. The nurse commented that the enema had been a failure, and left the room. I was left on my own and soon began to feel an urge to use the toilet. As I did so, I passed something hard and about the size of a golf-ball, together with some blood. Afterwards I reported this to the nurse.

Later that afternoon I was called down for the stretching procedure, and after recovery, the surgeon came to see me. He reported that no stretching had been necessary; that there was now no blockage and everything looked normal! I believe that God had intervened in a miraculous way in answer to prayer. At last, the way ahead seemed open for the reversal surgery and hernia repair to proceed. I received a date in September, with a verbal promise that I would definitely receive my surgery this time.

On the morning of September 7th, early in the morning, Maureen accompanied me to the hospital. This time the wait was short; everything looked positive; I prayed to God for success. The operation took place, and after recovery, I was returned to a small ward. By nightfall, when the ward lights were switched off, my mind was alert and I couldn't sleep. I lay in bed and talked to God in my thoughts and he talked back to me. He spoke to me like a loving Father who cared deeply for his child. He confirmed that I was on the road to healing and wholeness, such as I had never known before. He wanted me to learn childlike trust in all situations to replace fear and anxiety. Over the next day or two I continued to gain strength, and progressed onto light food. Then, unexpectedly, my condition deteriorated and I began to feel nauseous. I started vomiting green bile. My bowel had shut down completely. I was put on a drip. I felt sick and weak and hardly knew where I was, as my mind became confused. I could scarcely sleep and the nights seemed to last a lifetime. I could hardly pray to God, let alone sense his presence. Eventually, I began to stabilise. I was put on a nutritional feed through a tube in my neck, as I had been ten days without food.

At last, I began to sense God's Spirit with me once again. I received three separate impressions in my mind during this time. Firstly, I had a picture of shiny new parts which were waiting to be fitted to steam locomotive. A little later, I felt that I was a small child, sitting on God's lap, giggling and throwing rose petals in the air. Finally I saw myself as a man, dressed in armour, kneeling before the throne in heaven. I heard a voice speak to me and say; "Death wanted to take you, but I have fought for you. Now I have healed your wound and you will live."

The next day I received a visit from a professor from the psychiatric department. Due to the vomiting they had been forced to stop giving me lithium. Now this psychiatrist was asking me questions about my mental breakdown, nearly thirty years earlier, when I had first started on lithium. I opened my heart to him and told him the whole story about my homosexual inclinations; my male partner; my Christian conversion; my marriage; my suicidal letter and frightening experiences which led me to believe that I was doomed to hell. He listened intently, and seemed to believe and understand what I was saying and how I had felt. I was encouraged by his manner and empathy, and wondered how he would reply.

"It seems to me that you were overwhelmed by circumstances," he replied, "and a feeling of total failure. I do not believe that you are now bi-polar or a manic depressive. The lithium served you well at the time, but in my view is no longer necessary. I have decided to take you off lithium."

I had often asked God if I could stop taking lithium, but neither I nor the doctor had the courage to try. Now I had already stopped taking it for nearly two weeks, and I have had no ill effects since. Soon afterwards I was given the news that I was considered fit enough to go home to recuperate. Maureen came to collect me; I had been in hospital for over three weeks instead of the anticipated three to four days. Surely the times of testing were now over!

I arrived home on a Thursday, expecting to spend six to eight weeks recovering from my operation. I was very glad to be home. I unpacked my bag and ate a light supper, then settled into my bed, hoping for a good night's sleep. But before I could fall asleep, I had an urgent need to hurry to the toilet; after that, I was up and down to the toilet all night. I felt disappointed and concerned.

A "district nurse" was due to call daily at the house to change the dressing on the wound where the stoma had been. The nurse came on Friday lunch-time, and advised staying on a light diet for a further twenty-four hours. On Saturday, a second nurse called to dress the wound. She was concerned when I told her that I was now feeling sick and could only drink fluids. By Saturday night I felt nauseous and began to be sick again. On Sunday morning, the most senior nurse in the local team arrived at the house. I had just been sick, and a bowl of dark greenish liquid was still by my bedside! This nurse showed great concern about this, and after attending to my dressing, she phoned the "out of hours" service. Within an hour, an emergency doctor arrived and, after a brief examination, called for an ambulance. The ambulance arrived very quickly, and meanwhile, Maureen hurriedly re-packed a few items into my over-night bag. Two paramedics escorted me downstairs and into the waiting ambulance. I was taken straight up to an assessment ward. Silently, I was asking the Lord, "What's happening to me now?"

Once in the Assessment Ward, I was quickly put back onto a drip, and a tube was inserted up my nose to drain the bile. Once more I was labelled "nil-by-mouth" while tests were carried out. I had suffered a second shut-down of the bowel.

"Am I to go through another ten days of darkness and testing?" I asked myself. In the event, by Tuesday, I was started back on fluids and my family came to visit me, bringing me a large bottle of Lucozade. By Wednesday, I was allowed some solid food, but the doctors became alarmed as I began passing soft stools which were bright yellow. They were concerned that I might have contracted a contagious virus, and I was moved into an isolation room. I had my own washroom and toilet and Maureen was able to visit and pray with me in private. Whilst in this room, God's Spirit was able to minister to me more freely. That night, as I was worshipping, with my hands raised, I saw in a vision a great crowd of faces, like a cloud on the horizon. Amongst them, some faces stood out from the crowd, as I recognised people I had known who had died. These included my father, mother, and grandmother. I waved my arms while weeping tears of joy, and saw smiling faces and hands waving back at me. After the vision was over, I asked the Lord what it was that I had just seen. He replied; "These are a part of the "cloud of witnesses" spoken of in the Bible in Hebrews 12." Then I heard the Lord say to me; "You are now healed. It is time to publish your book."

By the following morning the doctors had decided that no dangerous virus was present. The bright yellow stools had been caused by colouring agents in the drink. That afternoon I was given the good news that I was now well enough to return home. Once again Maureen came to collect me.

During the first few days at home, I received what I might call a "honeymoon" period with the Lord. Each time I read the Bible, listened to worship music or prayed, I would again feel the presence of his Holy Spirit, often with tears of joy and excitement. After a few days of recovery at home, I began to prepare to write this story. As I looked back through my prayer journals from previous years, to my surprise, I came across an entry I had made in the year 2006, which was nine years earlier. It simply read: "When I have healed you, I want you to write a book of your testimony." I had completely forgotten about this word from the Lord.

Chapter 23

"Entering the Promised Land"

It is difficult to conclude a story which is still a work in progress. It has been over six months since my discharge from hospital last September. Since then I have also had my second hernia operation. At last my body has returned to its' normal condition.

Returning to the title of this story, "Coming out of homosexuality", I will briefly summarise in this chapter some very recent events, and my vision for the future. Then in the final chapter, I will offer the reader some "tips" from my own experience to maybe help you in your journey with the Lord.

I had by now recovered enough from my latest operation to have a soaking time with Maureen. As we held each-other and the music played, I felt a peace and oneness with my wife which had never been possible years before. I now feel more comfortable to be held in the arms of a woman and she is more able to be held in my arms. Although sexual attraction towards her is not present in a lustful way, the sense of revulsion which I used to get has now gone. The thought of engaging in sexual activity with another man now feels alien to me, even though the person may be attractive to look at. Something has changed within my thoughts and mind which I cannot adequately explain. It is not my doing; it can only be the changing work of God. If I turned away from God, would my former ways return? I do not know. I can only offer the reader my own experience as it is now. I feel confident that God has more to do in both of us, which will bring even greater freedom for romance and sexuality.

I had completed some basic training in TPM (Theophostic prayer ministry), over the previous year or so, and I have now embarked on training in "I.A." (Immanuel Approach). Both these are methods of emotional healing for trauma and hurts from the past. There can often be lies, spoken into us as children and adults, which have affected us and brought pain into our souls. From these can spring up addictions, unhelpful habits and bad reactions to current life events. I will give just one example:-

As a child, I was often told that "I was nothing but a lazy, fat, good-for-nothing pig." Strong words, and powerful! The result was that I grew up believing that I was lazy, unattractive and could never do anything right. I dreaded putting on weight as an adult and looking fat. The effect of these and other crushing comments reaped havoc with my self-worth, as can be seen from my story. I have forgiven my father for these and other harsh words, and recently, while in a healing session with a friend, I spoke to Jesus about these words which I had believed about myself. Then I asked him for his word of truth; how he felt about me. He replied that these words had been spoken out of my father's own brokenness, and that in the eyes of Jesus I was neither lazy nor good-for-nothing, but rather I was a sensitive person with a willing and obedient heart, and he was well pleased with me. Hearing these words from the Lord brought tears to my eyes and healing to my soul, and helped to free me up to be the man he had intended me to be.

Recently, I was watching an edition of a Christian television program called "It's Supernatural". The guest on this edition was the widow of Jack Frost, (of "Shiloh Ministries"). She shared about the transformation which took place in her late husband, a former alcoholic and control-freak, after receiving

Father-God's arms of love around him. I was moved by her testimony. Then the host of the program prayed a "father's blessing" over those watching. As he prayed this blessing, I found myself sobbing and weeping as the Lord brought further healing to my soul. The love of God fills the deep needs within us which otherwise crave to be filled by other things which do not satisfy. He has pronounced me healed from the past, yet he is continuing to bring about changes to my thinking and emotions. I have a greater peace and joy within my soul and a greater love for other people, and even for myself. I also feel a growing love and attraction towards my wife. After more than thirty years of marriage, romance is now beginning to blossom. I feel less like a wounded little boy and more like a man than ever before.

After years in the wilderness, I believe I am entering into the "Promised Land", a life of growing relationship and love for Father, Son and Holy Spirit. My desire is to reach out to the broken, the hurting and the lost with salvation, compassion and healing. In a way, whether a person has homosexual or heterosexual inclinations is incidental. God loves you just the way you are. You are a human being, created and loved by a wonderful God. You cannot change yourself by human effort, but you can find true meaning and purpose by surrendering your life and heart to God. Jesus died on the cross to take all our sins and sicknesses on his back, and he rose from the dead to win victory over death and the devil. Through him will come fullness of joy and healing of body, mind and spirit.

He will be your ***VERY GREAT REWARD***, both in this life and in the eternal life still to come!

Chapter 24

"Tips and Definitions."

Perhaps you've picked up this book with curiosity, and you've skipped straight to the last chapter to see if it's worth reading? Don't worry! That's something I often do too. If you want to peep at the ending, go back one chapter to number 23.

This final chapter is more like an appendix or summary of the Christian faith, offering some thoughts and definitions into subjects that might seem new to you or confusing. My story is especially relevant to those with same-sex attraction, but it is also suitable for a wider readership. Some readers may have no relationship with Jesus, while others may have known him for many years. The terms I use may be familiar to some and new to others. Above all, please bear in mind that we are all unique, and the way God works in your life will be different from the way he works in mine. The bottom line is: "He loves you and wants to bless you more than you can imagine!"

I know that attending church can be difficult for those who have suffered rejection and judgements in their lives. Fellowship is important for a believer in Christ, and there are many "web-churches" springing up on the internet. These can be exciting and powerful in content, and I watch some wonderful programs this way which have really blessed me. However, I highly recommend being part of a local church if that is possible for you. It is important to choose a place where you can feel wanted and loved. They say you can never find a perfect church, as all human beings are flawed in some way. However, there are great differences between different churches and it's important to find the right one for you, even if you have to try a few first. I list below some negatives and positives about typical churches in the UK. (Most fellowships are somewhere in between)

NEGATIVE	POSITIVE
Un-welcoming and distant.	Accepting and welcoming
Hypocritical and two-faced	Compassionate/Caring
Services boring and irrelevant	Lively worship/Reality
Rules and striving to perform	Freedom to express gifts
Out-of-date methods	Holy Spirit presence
Ungodly or faithless leadership	Bible-believing teaching
Diminishing congregation	Multi-ethnic/mixed-aged
Out-of-control spirituality	Well-ordered services

=========================

Now I offer my own understanding of some terms and definitions you may have read in this book, or may come across in church.

TRIUNE GODHEAD: [also referred to as the Trinity]

Christians believe in the Father, the Son (Jesus Christ) and the Holy Spirit. The great mystery is that they are "Three in One and One in Three." The Bible tells us that God the Father is eternal, everlasting, all-knowing and ever-present. You might say that he is the planner, designer and architect of everything in the universe. His son, Jesus, is also referred to as the "Word of God", and he spoke the word from God to everything that exists. He also came to us in human form 2000 years ago. The Holy Spirit is the third person in the Trinity, and he hovered over the Earth when everything was formless and empty, bringing into being the plan of God and the Word spoken by Jesus. The Holy Spirit was sent to live in the believers when Jesus had ascended into heaven after being crucified and raised from the dead. These three members of the Godhead are spirit-beings, and exist as three individual persons; yet they are in complete harmony with one-another in a bond of mutual love and total agreement. Therefore if we, in prayer, say that we have received a "picture" or a "word" from the Lord, it can be said to have come from God, Jesus or from Holy Spirit. They work together in unison. In my story I use these three names inter-changeably, and also refer to them collectively as, The Lord.

ANGELS AND DEMONS:

We read in the Bible, that God created other heavenly beings, before the Earth and mankind came into existence. We come across names like "archangel", "cherubim and seraphim", "living creatures", "twenty-four elders", etc., as well as angels of various types and sizes who serve God and man. The Bible also tells of an ancient rebellion in heaven, when an archangel named Lucifer wanted to become like God himself. He was thrown out of highest heaven with his supporting angels, [a third of the total number], and was renamed Satan, and his angels are now called fallen angels or demons. Satan took the guise of a serpent in the Garden of Eden when Adam and Eve were first created, and tricked them into eating the forbidden fruit from the Tree of Knowledge of good and evil. When mankind fell into this trap, Satan gained legal rights over the Earth and over mankind, and sin and disobedience to God entered the world. We still see today the outworking of evil in our world. But God had a master plan to redeem fallen mankind by sending into the world his son, Jesus, who lived without sin or blemish, died as a man, and was raised from the dead after three days, thus defeating the power of death and hell and offering mankind the opportunity to have his sins forgiven, believe in Christ, and be saved from hell to go to heaven.

WORSHIP:

As human beings, we worship God in various ways and with various expressions of love and adoration. Some enjoy loud and demonstrative ways of worship, while others prefer silent contemplation. Some enjoy modern songs with a worship band, while others like older hymns with organ accompaniment. God looks on our heart-attitude as we worship him and not on the style of worship. Our worship is not intended as a vehicle to flatter and appease a tyrannical and attention-seeking God, but rather to bring us into the presence of a loving father figure, who is at the same time an all-powerful awesome God, in order for him to bless us as we worship him.

JUSTIFICATION:

This term refers to our position before God, after the death and resurrection of Jesus Christ. He lived on Earth from a baby to an adult man, yet committed no evil. He died on the cross to carry the sins and sicknesses of all humanity for all time. His righteousness was exchanged for our sins, and when we believe in him by faith, we receive his righteousness before God the Father, irrespective of who we are and what wrong we have done. This is called justification, and is a free gift by "grace" from God. We have not earned this by good-works or self-effort, but by believing Christ's sacrifice made once and for all for every person.

SANCTIFICATION:

Having said that our righteousness is a free gift from God, even if we sin or turn away from him, he still sees us as justified and able to return into his presence through repentance. So we might ask; "is any behaviour, good or bad, acceptable to God?" If we love God, we will wish to please him by seeking his will for our lives and allowing him to gradually change ourselves and our habits through his mercy and grace. This process of change and growth in faith is called sanctification. It is his doing with our willingness, and should not be confused with "works of the flesh", which are our efforts to be good and holy in order to please other people or ourselves.

HEALING AND MIRACLES: Physical

This refers to healings received from God to our bodies. God can heal us through doctors, hospitals and medication, as well as the natural healing processes of the body. God can also heal our bodies through prayer, and such healing can be gradual or instantaneous. Supernatural healing can also take the form of "creative miracles," where something takes place which is beyond the skill of man. Such a miracle might be the growing out of a stunted limb into a fully-formed arm or leg; hand or foot. Or the replacement of worn-out or missing parts, such as a new kidney. God can even remove from our bodies, metal parts used by surgeons to repair damage, and replace them with new bone, muscle, nerves or sinews.

HEALING:- Emotional/mental

Examples of problems we may experience are listed below. I have listed them by heading only, without describing cause and effect:

(A) SINS COMMITED AGAINST US.

TYPE OF SIN OR EVENT	POSSIBLE OUTCOMES
Abuse: Physical, Emotional	Shame and Guilt
Slander and Gossip	Judgements and Vows
Anger and Rage	Depression/Anxiety
Rejection and Abandonment	Isolation/Addictions
Fear and Trauma	Fears and Phobias
Criticism and Cursing	Insecurity/Hopelessness

(B) SINS COMMITED BY YOU
(or passed down through the family line).

Pride, Lust, Greed, Envy, Laziness etc
Addictions and Bad habits
Un-forgiveness and Bitterness
Slander, Gossip and Judgements against others
Abuse against others: Physical, Mental or Emotional
Selfishness, Lies, Deceit, Rage, Murder
Idolatary, Witchcraft, Occult involvement

Many of these problems are present in all of us to some degree, and can be addressed through forgiveness, repentance, deliverance and through ministry of emotional healing.

I have mentioned a little of my own healing in the book, some of which came through prayer ministry. The truth is that in this fallen world, we all require some degree of healing, and can never attain the perfect state of wholeness before God which Jesus exhibited on Earth as a man. What can we do to become more healed?

GOD'S PART:

God has provided help for us to live as committed Christians. These include:

The Bible: This is the Word of God. As we read it and study it, we learn more about the nature of God and how he loved and dealt with his people, Israel. The Bible is as relevant today as when it was written. We can learn how to follow God's guidance, obey his will, and live in his love and protection.

Baptism in the Holy Spirit: This is the infilling by the Holy Spirit (as first recorded by the disciples of Jesus on the day of Pentecost).

Speaking in Tongues: This is the prayer language given supernaturally by the Holy Spirit to believers, which is useful for prayer and intersession, building up of the person in their faith and giving "messages-in-tongues" for interpretation. It is one of the "Gifts of the Holy Spirit" as set out in the Bible. [Other gifts include preaching, teaching, healing, prophesy, discerning of spirits, helps and encouragement.]

Forgiveness: If we repent (say sorry and turn from) our sins, God is faithful to forgive us our sins and cleanse us from all unrighteousness. However, there is a caution that we should also forgive those who have sinned against us. This can be difficult in certain instances, and we may need prayer-ministry and God's help to do it.

Deliverance: If we have consulted spiritualists and mediums; practiced any forms of witchcraft; received readings by tarot cards, ouija boards, horoscopes, etc, we have entered the realm of Satan and his demonic spirits, and we need to repent and renounce this. We may need to receive deliverance and prayer before being filled with the Holy Spirit.

OUR PART:

Our part in sanctification and growth in our faith and relationship with God includes a humble and contrite (willing) heart and fellowship with other Christians. The tools at our disposal are:

Bible reading/study: The Bible is the word of God for us to read and feed on in our hearts.

Prayer and intersession: Prayer is meant to be two-way communication with the Godhead. It is like oxygen to the believer. We ask and we believe to receive according to his will.

Praise and thanksgiving to God: It is good to give God our thanks and praise. We learn that all things work together for good for those who love God.

Water Baptism: This represents dying to self and washing away our past sins through water.

Soaking and meditating: This involves focusing on God and receiving from Holy Spirit peace, love, joy, healing etc.

Loving and serving: Not in our own strength or to impress others, but to obey God and his plan for our lives.

Fruit of the Spirit: The fruit of the Spirit are listed in the Bible. They grow gradually in us through the process of sanctification and include Love; Joy; Peace; Patience; Kindness, etc.

Giving and generosity: It is good to tithe a 10% portion of our income and be generous to those in need, through our time, abilities or finances.

===================

If you wish to seek further help or advice about sexually related subjects, here are some ministries you could contact:

www.truefreedomtrust.co.uk
www.livingout.org
www.genderplus.co.uk
www.livingwaters-uk.org
www.masteringlife.org
www.PurePassion.us
www.desertstream.org
www.exodusglobalalliance.org

Other ministries which I have found helpful in building my faith and walk with the Lord include:

www.xpministries .com
www.god.tv
www.sidroth.org
www.sidroth.org/its-supernatural-network
www.shilohplace.org
www.immanuelapproach.com
www.theophostic.com

May God bless you, and thank you for reading about my story.

#0074 - 240516 - C0 - 210/148/8 - PB - DID1463650